"Soong-Chan Rah explores the impact of ethnic and geographic shifts on the present and future state of evangelicalism. He gives us fair warning that parts of his heartfelt book are 'intended to provoke,' and they will. But that doesn't stop his book from being timely, thoughtful and very rewarding."

PHILIP JENKINS, Edwin Erle Sparks Professor of Humanities, Pennsylvania State University, and author of *The Next Christendom*

"In this manifesto for change, Soong-Chan Rah calls for the church to break free from limiting and exclusive paradigms and fully embrace the dramatic cultural diversity that is rapidly defining the twenty-first century in the United States. His powerfully persuasive pen engages and challenges the reader in ways that radically transform how church life is to be understood, shaped and lived."

CURTISS PAUL DEYOUNG, Professor of Reconciliation Studies, Bethel University

"Equal parts pastor, teacher and activist, Soong-Chan Rah sounds a loving but prophetic call for reform and reconciliation. His passion should not be misconstrued as condemnation. Rather, this book is about family business. May the evangelical community listen and grow."

EDWARD GILBREATH, editor, UrbanFaith.com, and author of *Reconciliation Blues*

"Soong-Chan Rah has a strong and prophetic message for the entire church regarding the changing face of Christianity in the United States and throughout the world. If we are going to be faithful to God's vision of extending his love to the entire planet, it will take leaders from every ethnic group fully empowered to lead. In *The Next Evangelicalism* Soong-Chan provides us with important insights to help us see this diverse kingdom vision become a reality."

NOEL CASTELLANOS, CEO, Christian Community Development Association

"Who will lead the way into the future? You may be surprised to know there is a rising group of third-culture, liminal citizens forging paths of influence in every sector of society. Soong-Chan Rah powerfully provokes us to take a hard look at our sins against the immigrants and this rising tide of next generation of Christ-followers representing many tribes and nations."

DAVE GIBBONS, founding pastor, Newsong

"Rah draws from the experiences of African American, Native American, immigrant and second-generation churches to free the church so that it can become the multicultural and holistic community that God has called it to be. *The Next Evangelicalism* is biblical prophecy at its best, summoning God's people to reconciliation, justice and faithfulness. As such, it is guaranteed at once to disturb, challenge, encourage and inspire."

F. Albert Tizon, Assistant Professor of Holistic Ministry, and director of Word & Deed Network, Palmer Theological Seminary

"Writing with uncanny nerve and refreshing candor, Rah 'captured' me from his first paragraph. . . . Rather than just describing the problem, Rah offers a biblically infused, socioculturally informed take on the future of evangelicalism that deserves to be taken seriously by us all."

Ken Fong, senior pastor, Evergreen Baptist Church of Los Angeles

"Soong-Chan Rah's *The Next Evangelicalism* is a book of amazing grace. It shows the American church how desperately blinded we are by Western colonization and white privilege. But more significantly, it helps us see God's liberation from this captivity and how he's using churches of the marginalized to set us free."

Russell Jeung, Associate Professor of Asian American Studies, San Francisco State University

"In this important book Soong-Chan Rah provides a compelling case that the dominant forms of North American Christianity have become enslaved by the patterns and assumptions of Western culture to the detriment of the gospel. Rah seeks to liberate the church from this cultural captivity by inviting readers to learn from the wisdom of communities that have generally been marginalized by the traditional church. The future of Christian witness in North America depends on listening to these voices and learning the lessons they have to teach."

John R. Franke, Clemens Professor of Missional Theology, Biblical Seminary

"Soong-Chan Rah's prophetic text is a must-read! This important book provides us both a serious biblical, theological, and sociocultural analysis and critique of the white church, while giving us a positive vision and models of the ever increasing nonwhite and ethnic church in America that we'd do well to emulate."

Eldin Villafañe, Professor of Christian Social Ethics, Gordon-Conwell Theological Seminary

The Next Evangelicalism

Releasing the Church from Western Cultural Captivity

Soong-Chan Rah

IVP Books

An imprint of InterVarsity Press
Downers Grove, Illinois

InterVarsity Press
P.O. Box 1400, Downers Grove, IL 60515-1426
World Wide Web: www.ivpress.com
E-mail: email@ivpress.com

InterVarsity Press® is the book-publishing division of InterVarsity Christian Fellowship/USA®, a
movement of students and faculty active on campus at hundreds of universities, colleges and schools of
nursing in the United States of America, and a member movement of the International Fellowship of
Evangelical Students.
For information about local and regional activities, write Public Relations Dept., InterVarsity Christian
Fellowship/USA, 6400 Schroeder Rd., P.O. Box 7895, Madison, WI 53707-7895, or visit the IVCF website
at <www.intervarsity.org>.

All Scripture quotations, unless otherwise indicated, are taken from the Holy Bible, Today's New
International Version™ Copyright © 2001 by International Bible Society. All rights reserved.

Design: Cindy Kiple
Images: Colman Lerner Gerardo/Shutterstock

ISBN 978-0-8308-3360-3

Printed in the United States of America ∞

Library of Congress Cataloging-in-Publication Data

Rah, Soong-Chan.
  The next evangelicalism: freeing the church from Western cultural
captivity / Soong-Chan Rah.
      p. cm.
  Includes bibliographical references.
  ISBN 978-0-8308-3360-3 (pbk.: alk paper)
  1. Evangelicalism—History—21st century. 2. Church history—21st
century. I. Title.
  BR1640.R34 2009
  270.8'3—dc22

                                                                              2008054478

P   18   17   16   15   14   13   12   11   10   9   8   7   6   5   4

Y   24   23   22   21   20   19   18   17   16   15   14   13   12   11   10

To my wife, Sue

God's gift and provision

To my children, Annah and Elijah

Helping me better understand God's delight

Contents

Acknowledgments

The journey of learning is never a solo venture. There are many names and faces that have shaped my thinking on these matters, but due to space considerations, some may go unmentioned.

I am indebted to my academic mentors. Doug and Judy Hall of the Emmanuel Gospel Center are truly an inspiration of faithfulness in ministry and in scholarship. Their research provided the initial spark for the writing of this book. My thanks to Dr. Eldin Villafañe, whose passion for justice I long to emulate. My thanks to Dr. Peter Cha, who has been both an academic and a personal mentor. Dr. Humberto Alfaro sparked my deeper exploration of urban theology.

I have been blessed with many wonderful models of ministry. My wife and I are indebted to Rev. Drs. Ray and Gloria Hammond, copastors of the Bethel A.M.E. Church in Boston, who walked alongside us when we were a young married couple in ministry. My thanks to Bishop Brian and Carmen Greene, Revs. Larry and Virginia Ward, Rev. Warren and Lynne Collins, Bil and Paulea Mooney-McCoy, and Nick and Sheila Rowe, who have been role models and examples in ministry and marriage. Dr. Ray Aldred and Rev. Dr. Terry LeBlanc have reshaped my ecclesiology and my theology from the framework of First Nations ministry.

I am grateful for my former church, the Cambridge Community Fellowship Church, which provided a safe place to explore these pressing issues. The congregation and the church leadership showed great generosity in affirming my passion to see God move in the next evangelicalism. The church also provided a model of what the next evangelicalism can and will look like. I have had the pleasure of working with a number of pastoral associates and seminary interns who have shaped and deepened my heart for multiethnic ministry. My gratitude to James Choung, Danny and Anita Colombara, Matt Lee, Jason Yung, Elizabeth Pierre, Gary VanderPol, Larry Kim, Vince Campbell, Diana Mojica, and many others who walked with me on this pastoral journey at CCFC.

North Park Theological Seminary has been a great landing place as I shifted from pastor to professor. The school has provided an academic community that continues to stretch my thinking and deepen my calling to serve the church. Thanks to our seminary president, Dr. Jay Phelan, who provided encouragement and feedback. Specific thanks to Dr. Paul DeNeui, who was helpful in reviewing key aspects of the manuscript, particularly chapter six. My teaching assistant, Jason Mach, provided invaluable support and help, not only by repeatedly reviewing the manuscript but also by providing key research and data. My thanks to Vicki Tsui, Ed Gilbreath, Helen Lee, Chris Brooks, Mae Cannon and the IVP readers who took the time to review the manuscript and provide valuable feedback. I am grateful to Jonathan Choe, who encouraged me to explore ways to promote the book using new media.

My expression of great thanks to InterVarsity Press, and particularly to my editor Al Hsu. I cannot think of a better person to chaperone me and hold my hand through my first solo project from beginning to end. I know that this book never would have gotten off the ground, much less have had a safe landing, if it were not for Al.

Finally, and most importantly, my family has been my strength and inspiration. Members of our extended family provided support and encouragement during the writing of this book. My children, Annah and Elijah, were always supportive of Daddy and were the best cheerleaders that a daddy could want. My wife, Sue, has been my inspiration and strength. God planted the seed for this work and caused it to grow, while my wife watered and cultivated it. She made tremendous sacrifices and provided a deep level of support that I could not have survived without. She has been God's gift to me that inspires me to push forward.

Introduction

AT THE CORNER OF MASSACHUSETTS AVENUE and Beacon Street in Boston sits an awe-inspiring building. The gray stone front and ornate stained glass are reminiscent of the glory years of a bygone era of the American church. It is the type of church building associated with the rich tradition of a church in New England. The first time I walked up to that corner, I couldn't help but be intimidated by what must be an impressive history for that church building. But when I turned the corner, I realized that the church building is literally a façade. Two of the outer walls of the church remain, but the actual church building behind the walls has been demolished and a luxury high-rise condo now inhabits the former sanctuary space. There is the external appearance of an historical church, but in reality that church is long since dead.

Throughout many cities in North America, there are numerous church structures that may have an impressive history but now host a very small group of worshipers on a Sunday morning. In Cambridge, there is a massive church building that dominates a central, busy intersection. In recent years, on a typical winter Sunday, that church will meet in a back room rather than in the main sanctuary. The church cannot afford the heat to meet in the thousand-plus person sanctuary. Nor would it be appropriate for a dozen or so elderly white women to meet in a thousand-plus person sanctuary. Within a half-mile radius of that

church, there are close to fifty churches (most of them immigrant, ethnic minority or multiethnic churches) that are crammed into much
smaller spaces. Right down the street from that large empty sanctuary
are over five hundred worshipers from five different congregations meeting in a small, cramped space—the host congregation of about forty
worshipers, a multiethnic congregation (with the largest group being
Asian American college students), a Haitian congregation, a Cape Ver-
dean congregation and a Friday-night gathering of Chinese international
students. The contrast between the large near-empty church building at
the busy intersection and the crowded smaller church building down
the street illustrates the reality of twenty-first-century American Christianity—the white churches are in decline while the immigrant, ethnic
and multiethnic churches are flourishing. As Dave Olson points out in
The American Church in Crisis, "The church in America is not booming.
It is in crisis. . . . As the American population continues to grow, the
church falls further and further behind. . . . Almost all of the data indicates that the church is fated to decline in influence every year in the
near future."[1]

As many lament the decline of Christianity in the United States in the
early stages of the twenty-first century, very few have recognized that
American Christianity may actually be growing, but in unexpected and
surprising ways.[2] The American church needs to face the inevitable and
prepare for the next stage of her history—we are looking at a nonwhite
majority, multiethnic American Christianity in the immediate future.
Unfortunately, despite these drastic demographic changes, American
evangelicalism remains enamored with an ecclesiology and a value system that reflect a dated and increasingly irrelevant cultural captivity
and are disconnected from both a global and a local reality.

A BOOMING GLOBAL CHRISTIANITY

One of the most significant developments in the new millennium is the
dramatic shift away from a northern and western hemisphere-centered
Christianity to a southern and eastern hemisphere-centered Christianity. As Philip Jenkins asserts in *The Next Christendom*: "Over the past

century [the twentieth century] . . . the center of gravity in the Christian world has shifted inexorably southward to Africa, Asia, and Latin America. . . . Christianity should enjoy a worldwide boom in the new century, but the vast majority of believers will be neither white nor European, nor Euro-American."[3]

Parallel to the undeniable reality of the changing demographics of global Christianity is the reality of Western Christianity's inability to grasp the implication of such dramatic changes. As Jenkins reveals, "Perhaps the most remarkable point about these potential conflicts is that the trends pointing toward them have registered so little on the consciousness of even well-informed Northern observers. What, after all, do most Americans know about the distribution of Christians worldwide? I suspect that most see Christianity very much as it was a century ago—a predominantly European and North American faith."[4]

Fifty years ago, if you were asked to describe a typical Christian in the world, you could confidently assert that person to be an upper middle-class, white male, living in an affluent and comfortable Midwest suburb. If you were to ask the same question today, that answer would more likely be a young Nigerian mother on the outskirts of Lagos, a university student in Seoul, South Korea, or a teenage boy in Mexico City. European and North American Christianity continue to decline, while African, Asian and Latin-American Christianity continue to increase dramatically. In the year 1900, Europe and North America comprised 82 percent of the world's Christian population. In 2005, Europe and North America comprised 39 percent of the world's Christian population with African, Asian and Latin American Christians making up 60 percent of the world's Christian population. By 2050, African, Asian and Latin American Christians will constitute 71 percent of the world's Christian population.[5] These numbers do not account for the fact that a majority of Christians in *North America* will be nonwhite. Global Christianity is clearly nonwhite. Thankfully, there is a growing recognition and an increasing awareness of these global changes. More literature is now available exploring global Christianity and its impact on missiology and theology.[6] But understanding the dramatic changes in Africa,

Asia and Latin America is only a part of the equation.

These changes are not only occurring globally, they are also occurring locally. Many sociologists predict that by the year 2050, the majority of U.S. residents will be nonwhite.[7] A U.S. Census Report in 2008 revealed that "minorities, now roughly one-third of the U.S. population, are expected to become the majority in 2042, with the nation projected to be 54 percent minority in 2050. By 2023, minorities will comprise more than half of all children."[8] The election of Barack Obama as the United States' first ethnic-minority president reveals the changing face of America. The public face of America is no longer a white male. Meanwhile, the trend of a nonwhite majority America will hit the churches faster than it will hit the general population. This trend is due in large part to the sustaining of American Christianity by newly arrived immigrants who bring their Christian faith with them. As sociologist R. Stephen Warner points out, "What many people have not heard . . . and need to hear is that the great majority of the newcomers are Christians. . . . This means that the new immigrants represent not the de-Christianization of American society but the de-Europeanization of American Christianity."[9] Contrary to popular opinion, the church is not dying in America; it is alive and well, but it is alive and well among the immigrant and ethnic minority communities and not among the majority white churches in the United States.

SHAPED BY EVANGELICALISM

My own story in coming to write this book is a result of my ongoing journey as a fellow pilgrim with other North American evangelicals. I was born in Seoul, South Korea—a nation bursting with spiritual renewal and church growth. It is a nation rapidly emerging as one of the epicenters for global evangelicalism. My family immigrated to the United States when I was six years old and encountered numerous difficulties as an immigrant family. There was the drop in social status and the economic struggles that almost all immigrant families face. I remember the shame of being on food stamps and the indignity of being laughed at by classmates because I was on the free school lunch program. For a significant portion of my childhood, we lived in a rough inner-city neighborhood in Baltimore. The neighborhood comprised poor whites, poor blacks and recent Korean immigrants. Racial misunderstanding and incidents were commonplace.

Coupled with (and maybe as a result of) the trauma of immigration were the numerous struggles and tensions within my family. The main source of stress came from my father's abandonment of our family when I was in elementary school. Now saddled with the responsibility of caring for four children in a foreign land, my mom's limited English curtailed her employment options. She ended up working two different jobs at the same time: a cook in an inner-city carryout during the day and a night shift nurse's aide in a senior citizens' home. She would work twenty hours a day, six days a week. My father's departure from our family meant that I lost both father and mother in one shot. In the midst of all these difficulties, it was an authentic Christian community that provided support and served as a lifesaver to our family. It was the church that gave our family stability and direction. It was an evangelical faith that transformed me from bitterness and defeat to an unwavering hope. I shudder to think who I would be without my evangelical faith.

I am a product of American evangelicalism. Much of what I believe, know and try to live out arises out of my involvement and development in the North American evangelical subculture. I grew up and found a personal faith in the context of a Korean immigrant church that tried to balance the best of the Korean homeland with the best of the "American" version of the Christian faith. I am steeped in the American education system—through elementary, secondary and higher education and the evangelical expressions within the educational system, such as InterVarsity Christian Fellowship, Gordon-Conwell Theological Seminary and North Park University. I have planted and pastored evangelical churches and have been and am currently a part of numerous evangelical small groups, networks, organizations and denominations. I currently teach at an evangelical seminary in training up future evangelical leaders. In many ways, evangelical Christianity defines my identity and status in American society.

Yet I am confronted with the reality of feeling marginalized in the context of my own faith tradition—that as immersed as I am in evangelicalism, I am oftentimes still seen as an outsider. In my journey as a neophyte believer, a youth pastor, a campus ministry participant, an emerging leader, a church planter, a local church pastor and a seminary professor, I have increased in my sense of frustration with the cultural captivity of the church. I grow weary of seeing Western, white expressions of the Christian faith being lifted up while failing to see nonwhite expressions of faith represented in meaningful ways in American evangelicalism. But as someone who loves the body of Christ, I long to see what immeasurably more God is able to do in the North American evangelical church.

THE NEXT EVANGELICALISM IS HERE

In the early 1990s I left my hometown in Maryland to begin seminary studies in New England. In preparing to move to the Boston area, my home church in Maryland took the time to pray that I would not lose my faith and spiritual passion in a region of the country that was perceived as spiritually dead. Every story that I heard or concern that was raised seemed to assume that the city of Boston represented the worst of a post-Christian region, and that secular humanism had completely overtaken that city.

But when I arrived in Boston I found a very different scenario. I found that Christianity was not only alive in Boston, it was flourishing. "From 2000 to 2005, the evangelical church grew in 28 states and declined in 22 states. . . . Massachusetts [was one of the five states that] had the greatest attendance percentage increase."[10] In 1970, the city of Boston was home to about 200 churches. Thirty years later, there were 412 churches. The net gain in the number of churches was in the growth of the number of churches in the ethnic and immigrant communities. "Since the first churches were started in the 1960s, more than 100 Spanish language congregations have been started in Boston. Beginning in 1969 the Haitian Christians began planting churches. More than 50 Haitian churches now serve the large Haitian population in greater Boston."[11] While only a handful of churches in 1970 held services in a language other than English, thirty years later, more than half of those churches held services in a language other than English.

Between 2001 and 2006, 98 new churches were planted in the city of Boston.[12] In a city the size of Boston, 98 new church plants in a six-year time period is not spiritual death, it is spiritual life and vitality. Why was it, then, that the majority of the country viewed Boston as a spiritually dead place? Of the 98 churches planted during that six-year time period, "76 of them reported the language of worship. Of those 76 churches, almost half of them . . . [have] non-English or bi-lingual [services], 19 worship in Spanish, 8 in Haitian Creole and 9 in Portuguese."[13]

In *The American Church in Crisis*, Olson notes that every region of the United States and every major Christian group (Catholic, mainline, evangelical) experienced a decline in total attendance between 1990 and 2005. The only group that saw a numerical increase was evangelicals in the Northeast region—due in large part to "the sharp increase in Asian, Hispanic, and other immigrant populations."[14] The perception nationally was that Boston was spiritually dead, because there was noticeable decline among the white Christian community. In contrast, there has been significant growth in the number of nonwhite Christians and churches in the Boston area.

At one point during my time in Boston, a group of very sincere young men and women came from a prayer group in the South to pray for revival in the city of Boston. They assumed that Boston was a spiritually dead and oppressed place. There was a sense of pity and concern expressed by these well-intentioned Christians for a pastor who was struggling in a city with such spiritual lifelessness. But that was not the Boston I knew. The Boston I knew was filled with vibrant and exciting churches. New churches were being planted throughout the city. Christian programs and ministries were booming in the city. But this spiritual vitality was not as evident among the white churches. The spiritual energy and dynamism in the city centered on the multiethnic, immigrant and ethnic minority churches. The work of the Boston Ten-Point Coalition (composed mostly of African American clergy) stifled youth-related violence throughout Boston. Haitian churches were involved in an effort to bring justice and fairness to nursing home workers. A Latino pastor and an African American bishop led the Christian community in spiritual revival for the city and for political change. Church planting efforts among Asian American young adults and campus ministries composed of Asian Americans flourished throughout Cambridge/ Boston. Boston is alive with spiritual revival, particularly among the ethnic minority communities. But very few seem to recognize this reality, even as this trend begins to appear nationally.

THE WHITE CAPTIVITY OF AMERICAN EVANGELICALISM

While the demographics of Christianity are changing both globally and locally, the leadership of American evangelicalism continues to be dominated by white Americans. During my years as a senior pastor of a local church, not a week would go by without my receiving an invitation to some sort of pastors' conference. These national conferences would gather together the "experts" and the key leaders of American evangelicalism. Of the fifty-plus speakers (platform or workshop) scheduled for these conferences, there may have been one African American platform speaker and maybe one other nonwhite leading a workshop, but the rest of the speakers would be white. What is the message? The real experts in ministry are whites. Nonwhites may offer some expertise in specialized areas of ministry (such as urban ministry or racial reconciliation), but the theologians, the general experts, the real shapers and movers of ministry, are whites.

In February of 2005, *Time* magazine profiled the twenty-five most influential evangelicals in the United States. Only two of those slots were occupied by nonwhites.[15] Initially I was quite upset at *Time* magazine for having so few nonwhites on that list. But eventually I came to accept that, in this case, the media was actually reporting the news rather than creating it. *Time's* perception of who represents and leads American evangelicalism was a fairly accurate portrayal. While the demographics of American Christianity are changing, the perceived and acknowledged leadership of American Christianity remains white.

The *Wall Street Journal* recognized the changing demographic in American Christianity and responded to the *Time* article:

Time Magazine built a recent cover story around its list of the 25 most influential evangelicals. The list features a fair number of success-driven entrepreneurs whose achievements can be measured by standards that Time writers understand—book sales, converts, market share. Time's evangelicals of influence are Anglo (23 of 25). . . . But this traditional face of American evangelicalism is changing. An ever higher number of U.S. evangelicals—perhaps nearing a third of the total—are Asian, African, Latin American or Pacific Islander. . . . The 20th-century global explosion of evangelicalism has come full circle: Evangelicals from everywhere rub shoulders in the U.S. Not that the media have really noticed.[16]

Both *Time* and the *Wall Street Journal* had it right. The acknowledged leadership of American evangelicalism is white, but the face of American evangelicalism is now multiracial.

In the last few years, I have had the opportunity to visit and speak at a number of different Christian colleges, oftentimes to speak on the topic of racial reconciliation and multiethnicity. I raise the question that, given the changes in demographics in both global and American Christianity, why are there not more minority faculty members at these Christian colleges and seminaries? There may be a handful of minority faculty members at these Christian schools, but usually no more than that. The few ethnic minority faculty members will often be held up as examples of the school's progress toward diversity. However, most institutions face great difficulty moving beyond the one or two minority hires. The consistently poor record of minority faculty hires at Christian colleges and seminaries is not only disappointing, it is irresponsible. Among evangelical seminaries, the percentage of nonwhite student enrollment has increased from approximately 15 percent in 1977 to 31 percent in 2005. However the percentage of faculty of color in 2005 stood at 12 percent,[17] which is disproportionally and significantly lower than the 31 percent minority student enrollment.

Furthermore, the last available study on the percentage of minority faculty at evangelical Christian colleges and universities, conducted in 1998, shows that minority faculty made up only 3.6 percent of Christian college faculty, which was actually a drop from the percentage of minority faculty in 1995.[18] A random sampling of twenty different Christian colleges and evangelical seminaries provided by the *Chronicle of Higher Education* in 2007 reveals that ethnic minorities comprise less than 7 percent of the faculty at those twenty schools.[19] If these schools are indeed preparing leaders for the next generation, then for their students to have limited or no exposure to minority faculty mentors is to shortchange their education.

What is even more distressing is that institutes of Christian higher education oftentimes set the theological agenda for the American church. So while the demographics of American evangelicalism are undergoing dramatic change, the theological formation and dialogue remains captive to white Christianity. What we are witnessing in the twenty-first century is the captivity of the church to the dominant Western culture and white leadership, which is in stark contrast to the demographic reality of Christianity in the twenty-first century. Even if we could justify the white captivity of the church in the early part of the twentieth century, there is no justification for it now.

THE DEBILITATING POWER OF CULTURAL CAPTIVITY

What is Jesus' heart for the church? I once heard the perspective that Almighty God has had to endure three indignities in human history. The first indignity was Adam and Eve's disobedience and rejection of YHWH in the Garden of Eden. The second indignity was Jesus' suffering and public humiliation on the cross. And the third indignity was that he trusted his name to a group of humans (the church) that have brought humiliation and indignity to the holy name of Jesus. This ongoing humiliation requires repentance and reformation. We need repentance from our cultural captivity and a willingness to reform our church in the next era of North American evangelicalism.

For most of its history (but particularly in the last fifty years), American evangelicalism has more accurately reflected the values, culture and ethos of Western, white American culture than the values of Scripture. At times, the evangelical church has been indistinguishable from Western, white American culture. In the emerging culture and the next evangelicalism of the twenty-first century, we must consider how evangelicalism has been held captive to Western, white culture and explore ways that the Christian community can reflect biblical more than cultural norms. Where is the church that will uphold the name of Jesus? Where is the pure and holy bride that Jesus longs to return for? Currently, we are seeing the Western, white captivity of the American evangelical church, but we can hope that it is time for a new era of the church in the next evangelicalism.

In church history, the phrase "captivity of the church" has been used in different contexts with varied meanings. In the context of the Protestant Reformation, Martin Luther wrote the tract *On the Babylonian Captivity of the Church*,[20] likening the Catholic Church's stranglehold on the sacraments to the capture and exile of the Israelites by the Babylonians. To Luther, the church's lack of understanding and application of faith and grace revealed a doctrinal captivity of the church. Luther asserts that the medieval Catholic Church held little resemblance to the characteristics of the community of God found in Scripture.

In more recent years, R. C. Sproul has written the "Pelagian Captivity of the Evangelical Church,"[21] about a church that is held captive by the Pelagian view of the basic goodness of humanity rather than reflecting Scriptural perspectives on original sin and human fallenness. Authors such as H. Richard Niebuhr, Lesslie Newbigin, Stanley Hauerwaus, Rodney Clapp and others have written about the relationship between the church and the culture—employing concepts that speak to the potential danger of the church's captivity to the culture around it. *Total Truth* by Nancy Pearcey is an attempt at "liberating Christianity from its cultural captivity." Gibson Winter seeks to address the *Suburban Captivity of the Churches*, while Cornel West alludes to a Constantinian captivity of Christianity.[22]

The phrase "captivity of the church" points to the danger of the church being defined by an influence other than the Scriptures. The church remains the church, but we more accurately reflect the culture around us rather than the characteristics of the bride of Christ. We are held captive to the culture that surrounds us. To speak of the white captivity of the church is an acknowledgement that white culture has dominated, shaped and captured Christianity in the United States. At times, the white evangelical church has been enmeshed with Western, white American culture to the great detriment of the spread of the gospel. This state of American evangelicalism cannot continue if we are to move toward the future of a next evangelicalism.

In some portions of the book, I will use the term *white* captivity as a synonym for *Western* captivity. In my description of the white captivity of the church (individualism in chapter one and materialism/consumerism in chapter two), many of these attributes may appear more simply to be characteristics of Western culture, rather than specifically of white America. The phrase "white captivity of the church" is used to remind us that Western culture has been dominated by whites throughout its history. It is also used to help us distinguish the significant role of racism in Western culture and subsequently, American Christianity (chapter three). A significant oversight that will be confessed from the onset is that, in our focus on the issue of race in this work, we will not invest the necessary time and effort to discuss the white *male* captivity of the American evangelical church. We must recognize, however, that the issue of gender captivity also plays a prominent role in the cultural captivity of the church.

The Western, white captivity of the church is most evident in examples like the church growth movement of the latter half of the twentieth century (chapter four) and even evident in a new thing like the emerging church (chapter five). But surprisingly, it is now finding its strongest and most visible expression in many non-Western cultural contexts (chapter six). Breaking through the white captivity of the church will be a difficult task, but with the dawning of the next evangelicalism, change must come. The change that must come may find its inspiration from nonwhite expressions of Christianity in the United States: the African American church of the Civil Rights movement and the contextualized theology emerging out of the Native American Christian community provide a model of a prophetic church confronting racism and breaking the barriers of power and privilege (chapter seven); the holistic expression of evangelism as reflected in the immigrant church in contrast to the materialism of the church growth movement (chapter eight); and the liminal, bicultural expression of multicultural community developing among the second-generation progeny of immigrants (chapter nine). These examples will provide a template and model of best practices for the next evangelicalism.

There are portions of the book that are intended to provoke. There may be times when the reader may react with anger, derision, defensiveness and so forth. But as you read through the major arguments of this book, I hope you will find my deepest concern for the church, the body of Christ and the pure and holy bride of Jesus. The tone of this book will at times seem angry and confrontational. There may be aspects of this book that cause discomfort. Confrontation can lead to discomfort, but confrontation and discomfort can also lead to transformation. After all, without a disturbed sense about ourselves,[23] why would anyone change?

The true intention of the book is to bring reconciliation and renewal to the church in America—confronted with its past, concerned about its present and confused about its future. I believe in the future of the church. It is not a hope based upon what I see in the now, but in the promise of the not yet—the promise that what Christians have repeatedly damaged, Christ is able to restore and to heal. It is for the church that Jesus was willing to lay down his life. It is for the church that Jesus longs to return. It is for the church that Jesus has a greater promise beyond Western, white cultural captivity.

PART ONE

The Western, White Cultural Captivity of the Church

1

Individualism

The Heartbeat of Western, White Cultural Captivity

KELLY ENTERED THE WORSHIP SERVICE with great expectations. The past week had been filled with disappointments. Her husband had been preoccupied and inattentive. Her three elementary-aged children had been acting up all week. Every day of the week had been an exercise in testing her patience. Throughout the week, she had been unable to find time to pray or to read the Bible. About two months back, she and her husband had stopped attending their small group meetings. Her husband had lost interest a long time ago, and she was getting weary of hearing about the crisis of the week from various members of the group. Everyone politely nodded their heads as they shared their weekly woes, but nobody was sure if they were nodding their heads in agreement and sympathy or were subtly asking the person sharing to hurry along. The Bible was hardly opened as the group spent most of their time hearing individual stories of struggle.

Her church had been her solace in so many different ways, and she was hoping for a bit more this Sunday morning. The worship team kicked off with a few of her favorite songs, with lyrics that reflected her personal faith, such as: "Here I am to worship, here I am to bow down." / "I have a living hope, I have a future, God has a plan for me, of this I'm sure." / "Your grace is enough for me." When the pastor preached that morning, his sermon spoke to her personal need for spiritual renewal. God is *her* God, able to meet *her* needs, and wanting to be *her* Savior. The closing worship song ("My Savior loves, my Savior lives, my Savior has always been with me") punctuated the power of God to meet her personal and individual needs.

As she departed the service, however, she felt a bit of a letdown. She greeted the pastor warmly but felt that he had disappointed her somehow. The sermon had scratched her itch but had not addressed the source of her itch. Her world still felt small and her God still felt small—a God limited to the personal realm of her life, rather than a big God able to transcend her seemingly small world. The God of her church was only as big as the individuals in the church and the personal needs of those individuals.

As a pastor, I am often confronted with the sense of letting down a congregation that is expecting a personalized worship service that ministers specifically to the individual member. In the formation of the Sunday worship service, I realize that I often fail to meet the expectations of the individual members of my congregation. On Monday mornings, I often picture the faces of individual members who were disappointed that I did not speak to their specific need for that week. I am also aware that even if I make every effort to meet every personal and individual need, someone will still not have had his or her personal needs met. Maybe a larger and more important question is: why am I trying so hard to meet the specific and personal needs of the individual? What drives me to see the church not as the expression of God's kingdom but merely as a forum to address individual needs?

ME, MYSELF AND I: THE UNHOLY TRINITY OF WESTERN PHILOSOPHY

A few years ago, our family was packing for our move from Cambridge, Massachusetts, to Chicago. I hate moving, but I actually enjoyed the process of culling through and categorizing my collection of books. During this process, I stumbled across an intriguing little book called

Philosophy for Beginners.[1] The book traces the entire history of Western philosophical thought in comic book form. For instance, Nietzsche is portrayed as a superhero (or more accurately as an *Übermensch*), Daffy Duck narrates the discourse on Hegel, and so forth. So before packing the book for the movers, I decided to read through it to get the comic book overview of Western philosophy. Interestingly, even a comic book was able to discern the central theme of Western philosophy: individualism.

From Hellenistic philosophy to medieval thought to the Enlightenment and postmodernity, each phase of Western philosophy has put forth as its central tenet the primacy of the individual. Whether it is Plato's philosopher hero emerging from the cave of shadows on his own accord, Rousseau's prioritizing of the individual in the application of the social contract, the "majority of one" advocated by the residents of Walden Pond, Ayn Rand's contention of the redemptive value for society of an individual's selfish egoism or the individualistic reading of Jacques Derrida's deconstructionism—regardless of the philosopher's context, the repeating motif of Western culture has been the centrality and primacy of the individual.

Numerous social analyses of American culture reveal our obsession with the individual and our struggle with the effects of an individual-focused worldview. One of the earliest assessments of American society comes from Alexis de Tocqueville in *Democracy in America.*[2] The French academic postulated that the then-young nation would struggle balancing strong individualistic tendencies with the collectivism required by a democratic form of government. In reflecting on Tocqueville, Herbert Gans asserts that "the United States has changed only slightly in over 150 years, and one of the stable elements is the continued pursuit of individualism by virtually all sectors of the population."[3] From the earliest stages of American history, individualism has been the defining attribute in understanding our nation's ethos.

The American church, in taking its cues from Western, white culture, has placed at the center of its theology and ecclesiology the primacy of the individual. The cultural captivity of the church has meant that the church is more likely to reflect the individualism of Western philosophy than the value of community found in Scripture. The individualistic philosophy that has shaped Western society, and consequently shaped the American church, reduces Christian faith to a personal, private and individual faith.

FUNDAMENTALISM, EVANGELICALISM AND INDIVIDUALISM

Late twentieth-century evangelicalism owes much of its formation and shape to early twentieth-century fundamentalism, which prioritized individualism at the cost of recognizing the corporate nature and corporate role of Christianity. This emphasis arose out of the cultural norms of American society. Historian George Marsden describes the religious individualism that reflects a central element of fundamentalism. "The individual stood alone before God; his choices were decisive. The church, while important as a supportive community, was made up of free individuals."[4] Despite its claims of separation from larger cultural influences, fundamentalism built its theological foundation on the central cultural influence of individualism.

The evangelical successors to fundamentalism continued to prioritize individualism as a primary expression. Paul Metzger in *Consuming Jesus* addresses the role of individualism as the thread linking fundamentalism and evangelicalism. Metzger notices how the two movements are bound up in the "privatization of spirituality, dissolution of public faith, and loss of an extensive, overarching social consciousness."[5] Less enamored with hard-line doctrinal positions, evangelicals were even more susceptible to cultural captivity and acquiescence to larger cultural influences. "As American evangelicals, we prize the individual and personal relationships. . . . The Bible has much to say about the importance of the individual, personal responsibility, and the need for [personal] evangelism."[6] A personalism and a prioritizing of the individual can be found at the sociohistorical roots of evangelicalism. Life and ministry in the local church, therefore, became the race to please the individual so that the pews might be filled.

INDIVIDUATION VS. INDIVIDUALISM

It is important at this time to make the distinction between the negative impact of an *excessive* individualism found in Western culture versus the healthy role of individuation. Individuation is a valuable Western philosophical, psychological contribution which allows for the healthy and necessary differentiation of the individual from family/society/culture/people groups/nations. Individuation allows individuals to grow up and make their own decisions—not based solely upon the pressures of society. Individuation allows for an important and necessary process of developing a personal relationship with Jesus. Individuation, therefore, reveals an important aspect of the individual expressions of faith and the need for individual salvation. God is not only a transcendent God that is beyond our comprehension, God is also an immanent God—nearby, close and personal. The individuation of our relationship with God and the personal appropriation of God's grace are crucial developments of Christian faith.

In my last year in seminary, I was facing a crisis of calling. I was struggling with a deep sense of inadequacy that I would be unable to fulfill my calling as a pastor. During my years at seminary, I had begun to formulate a list of my inadequacies and all of the ways that I did not live up to God's expectations. I was operating under a covenant of works in order to fulfill my calling as a pastor. The formation of this mental list led me to the conclusion that I should not pursue a pastoral calling. The grace of God was an abstract concept removed from my personal reality. The grace of God had not been able to break through the barrier of my personal history.

When my father left our family when I was in elementary school, we did not hear from him for several years. One day, seemingly out of the blue, I received a phone call from my father. Without too much formality he began to ask me a series of questions. "Are you getting straight A's in school?" "What level math are you in?" "Who's your favorite Renaissance artist?" (I think I said Picasso.) I was on the phone for over ten minutes as my father asked me a series of questions. At the end of the phone call, my ten-year-old mind had formulated a conclusion. I have to earn my father's love. If I want my father to love me, then I need to fulfill the list of achievements and accomplishments he had listed. When I got off the phone, I went to my room and cried.

After that phone call, I began to live out that conversation and internalized the pressure to achieve in order to earn my father's love. My personal identity and self-perception were shaped by an absent father's expectations. So I got A's in school and excelled academically. I got degrees from Ivy League schools. I did the things that I thought would earn my earthly father's love. Concurrently, I began to look for ways to earn my spiritual Father's love. I led my church's youth group, I participated in my church's evangelistic outreach programs and short-term mission trips, I became involved in campus ministry, I even attended seminary. But the list of "must do to earn my Father's love" kept getting longer and longer. Eventually this list became a list of my failures.

I have no doubt that in my last year in seminary, the emotional impact of that phone call was still affecting me and playing out in my formation of a list of failures before God. I could not be a good pastor because of all the ways I did not live up to my heavenly Father's expectations. It was around that time that I attended a conference that was held in Toronto. After the sermon a group of people went around and prayed for individuals. I knelt nearby to pray and I began to rehearse the list of failures in my mind. I began to bargain with God, reviewing the list of my personal failures. "God, how could I ever serve you when my list of failures is so long?" It was at that moment that I heard God speaking: "What list are you talking about?" God had not kept any record of wrongs. No list of failures existed. As people gathered around me to pray, instead of being overwhelmed by tears of guilt, I was flooded with joyful laughter.

I needed to know that my God was a personal God that cared about me as an individual, whose love for me was not based upon the expectations of others. Through my evangelical experience I was exposed to the power of grace appropriated on a personal level. I am personally indebted to Western culture's expression of an individual faith. Without it, my Christian worldview would not have an opening to the importance of knowing and being loves by a personal God that loves me as an individual. One of Western Christianity's greatest contributions is the possibility of experiencing the grace of God on a personal and individual level.

However, this individuation does not need to occur at the expense of an appreciation of a corporate point of view. Excessive and hyper-individualism contrasts to the healthy process of individuation by enslaving the individual to the tyranny of individualism, leading to personalism and privatism. The danger of the Western, white captivity of the church is an excessive individualism and personalism that reflects the narcissism of American culture rather than the redemptive power of the gospel message.

The Bible and Me

The priority of the individual shapes how American evangelicals live out our local church experience, how we study and learn Scripture, how we shape our corporate worship and even how we live and interact in community. For example, our Bible studies become the search for a personal and individualized understanding. If we were to pay attention to the intended audience of the various books of the Bible, we would find that only a handful of books were actually written exclusively to individuals—such as 2 Timothy, Titus, Philemon. An overwhelming number of books in the Bible are written to communities: the people of God, the nation of Israel, the church in Colosse and Corinth, the seven churches in Asia Minor, etc. Yet, why is it that our reading of the text centers so much on the individual reading of Scripture versus a corporate reading as the overwhelming majority of the Scriptures demand?

In a typical American church, are we taking teaching intended for the community of faith and reducing it to an application exclusively on an individual level? Our Sunday sermons emphasize how the individual can live his or her best life or how to have a purpose and direction from Scripture for his or her personal life by claiming the promises of a specific prayer for the individual. Too few Sunday sermons focus on how the community is called to respond to social problems or to reflect a corporate identity as God's people.

The Western hermeneutic of Scripture relies upon an individual focus and an individual application. Individualism dictates not only *what* we preach, but *how* we preach. In recent years, narrative preaching has come into vogue. More and more preachers are exploring the lost art of storytelling as a means of communication. The power of storytelling is in the way it can move beyond the individual experience to a community experience. Stories have the power to change cultures and social systems. But because our individualism is so deeply embedded, even that genre of preaching gets reduced to a series of propositions and an individualized, personalized application.

I was at a pastors' conference on the inner life of the Christian. The main speaker was very good at telling stories of his own life and stories of pastors he had mentored. The stories were gripping and moving. If he had just told the story and allowed the Spirit of God to move through the story, his teaching would have left a more favorable impression on me. But at the end of each story, he insisted on "explaining" the story to us so that we got the main point, that is, the propositional truth embedded in the story. At the end of one particular story, his propositional application was that we should vote a politically conservative agenda if we wanted to fulfill our spiritual calling. He had taken beautiful and powerful stories and reduced them to a Republican agenda that I could specifically apply in my individual life by voting his personal agenda. Even if the forms of our sermons change, they still remain individualized applications for the most important subject of the Bible: me.

Scripture does speak to an individual faith and the possibility of a personal relationship with Jesus. In the Gospels, Jesus is intentional and deliberate about addressing individuals on a personal level. He interacts with Zaccheus not merely as a corrupt member of a warped society, but as an individual in need of redemption. He connects with the adulterous woman, not simply as a creation of social structures but as an individual deserving of grace. Jesus is very personal in his interactions. However, to reduce Jesus' teachings and his life to merely an individual expression is to do disservice to the full canon of Scripture. The doctrine of the incarnation reveals that Jesus is a personal God; however, Jesus' incarnation is a heavenly invasion that has a social as well as an individual implication. Jesus comes announcing the kingdom of God, not merely expressed on an individual level but also on a societal level.

Reading Scripture from only an individual perspective and framework allows for a number of different misinterpretations and misapplication of God's Word. For example, Christians often cite Jeremiah 29:11, "'For I know the plans I have for you,' declares the LORD, 'plans to prosper you and not to harm you, plans to give you hope and a future,'" as an expression of comfort for the individual going through a difficult time. Many Christians assume that the "you" of this passage is singular and that this passage holds a promise of a better life for the individual. In actuality, the "you" of this passage is plural and the direction of this passage is to speak of a corporate, not a personal, blessing for the people of God.[7] Our individualized theology limits how we understand Scripture: rather than living out scriptural truths we focus on an interpretation of Scripture that caters to the needs of the individual.

It's All About Me . . . and All This Is for Me

In another important area of church life, the worship life of the congregation, the Western priority of the individual determines the approach to worship over the biblical guidelines for worship. Worship in the white captivity of the church is oftentimes a collection of individuals who happen to be in the same room. Worship is just between the individual and God, and the church service exists to help facilitate that individual communion.

Many years ago, I was the worship leader for a church that used contemporary worship songs. Back then (before the ubiquitous use of PowerPoint and LCD projectors), we had transparencies placed on an overhead projector. There would be a designated individual in charge of the large box of overheads, which were filed in alphabetical order based upon the first line or title of the song. The file folder containing the songs that began with the letter *A*, *J* or *G* (as well as most of the other letters of the alphabet) would be fairly thin—songs like "Awesome God" / "Jesus, You Are Lord" / "God Is so Good"—but the one folder that seemed to contain half of the songs in the transparency box was the folder of songs that began with the letter *I*. While there are times when we should express our personal adoration of God, should the subject of the majority of our songs be the great *I* rather than the great I AM? Worship, which should be the ascribing of worth to an Almighty God, becomes an exercise of attaining a personal self-fulfillment.

Christopher Lasch's assessment of American culture is best described by the title of his book *The Culture of Narcissism*. In this book Lasch employs the phrase "the third great awakening," an ironic phrase considering that the first two great awakenings in America involved major spiritual revival. Lasch describes this third great awakening as a therapeutic experience, not a religious one. "People today hunger not for personal salvation, let alone for the restoration of an earlier golden age, but for the feeling, the momentary illusion, of personal well-being, health, and psychic security."[8]

Our overreliance on therapeutic culture is a reflection of excessive individualism—the desire to have one's personal needs met with the focus of an entire hour being upon the individual. Therapeutic culture that arises out of an excessive individualistic focus yields a narcissistic focus in American society. This narcissistic individualism, of American society finds a direct corollary in the American evangelical church. Our church life becomes an expression of an individualism, yielding a self-absorbed narcissism. Instead of the church becoming an expression of a spiritual life lived in the community of believers or a spiritual life expressed in the context of a neighborhood community, our church life becomes a fulfillment of our individual desires and needs. Elements of the worship service, including the preaching of the Word and the worship of God, become reduced to a form of therapy that places the individual at the center of the worship service.

Excessive individualism in American society yields, therefore, the loss of community life. Robert Putnam, in *Bowling Alone*, describes American society as becoming increasingly disconnected and lacking in the important value of social capital. "Voting in America is down by about a quarter, and interest in public affairs by about one-fifth, over the last two or three decades."[9] In nearly every area of social life and using various measurements of civic involvement (such as serving as an officer in a club, serving on a committee in a local organization, writing a congressperson, signing a petition or attending a public town or school meeting), there is significant decline. Putnam characterizes this phenomenon through the motif of bowling alone—an individualized social activity. "More Americans are bowling than ever before, but league bowling has plummeted. . . . a profile that precisely matches the [declining] trends in other forms of social capital."[10] The image of bowling alone reflects the decline of social capital and connection, which arises out of the excessive individualism that dominates American culture. Consistently, we see that the central characteristic of American society is shaped by the philosophy of the primacy of the individual over and above the community. Individualism guides the American way of life.

The individualized narcissism of our society translates into our church life in not only our self-absorbed worship and our longing for sermons that speak to us or bless us personally but even in how we live out our church community life. A therapeutic culture translates into the context of the local church with an individualized and personalized approach to counseling and self-care. Community is lost in the process of a highly individualized approach. Even small group ministry, which is supposed to be the primary expression of community life in the American evangelical church, often yields a narcissistic, individualistic focus. Small groups become a place of support and counsel rather than a place where Scripture challenges the participants toward kingdom living. They can feel more like support groups rather than a place of spiritual growth. As the authors of *Habits of the Heart* point out: "Almost the only groups that are growing are the support groups. . . . These groups make minimal demands on their members and are oriented primarily to the needs of individuals: indeed [they involve] individuals who focus on themselves in the presence of others, what we might call being alone together."[11] How we approach counseling in the church is a highly individualized approach reflecting a personalized psychology.

The personalized psychology of American culture is counterproductive in the long run. When the self becomes the focus of nearly every element of human life and cultural expression, the community begins to die. Sociologist Richard Sennett reveals Western culture's priorities by stating:

> Each person's self has become his principal burden; to know oneself has become an end, instead of a means through which one knows the world. And precisely because we are so self-absorbed, it is extremely difficult for us to arrive at a private principle, to give any clear account to ourselves or to others of what our personalities are. The reason is that, the more privatized the psyche, the less it is stimulated, and the more difficult it is for us to feel or to express feeling.[12]

This excessive emphasis on individualism is crippling to American society, but even more so to the body of Christ.

Is there a possibility of restoring a sense of community to our approach to church life? A significant part of expanding our framework away from the individual worldview is experiencing multiethnic and multicultural worship, allowing us to see worship expressed in the context of the next evangelicalism rather than merely in the context of the Western, white captivity of the church. More and more individuals are seeing the importance and necessity of a crosscultural experience in moving beyond the self-absorption of individualism to experiencing a community of faith in the context of a crosscultural community.

In our worship setting, we need to see more of a corporate and community call to worship. Even the simple act of changing the "I" focused to "we" focused songs can signal a shift to the congregation. Our preaching and worship should direct our attention toward a God greater than our own experience. Recently, I visited a church that made a conscious effort in their worship service to direct attention toward the needs of others in the choosing of liturgy and the selection of worship songs. The prayers offered focused on prayers for the community and neighborhood. The call to confession incorporated corporate confession as well as individual confession. Churches can also reexamine the intention of small group gatherings to determine if the groups exist for the affirming of individualism or the building of community. One of the ways a church can build community is by accepting the weaknesses and shortcomings of others.

During a training seminar for our small group leaders, a scenario was raised by one of our leaders. She was concerned about an individual in the group who was struggling with a very difficult issue. The problem was that the leader felt that the issue was beyond her scope of expertise and the fact that the same issue came up week after week was now proving to be a distraction to the other members in her group. The small group leader's first reaction was to ask the pastor to intervene and remove the individual from the group context. My first reaction as the pastor was to refer this individual as soon as possible to a professional counselor. Both the small group leader and I were seeing the individual need rather than the power of life in community.

Noted Christian counselor Larry Crabb speaks about the need to move Christian counseling and pastoral care out of the realm of an exclusive professionalism toward a model of counseling in community.[13] Crabb proposes that "communities of God's people, ordinary Christians whose lives regularly intersect, will accomplish most of the good that we now depend on mental health professionals to provide."[14] The counseling needs of the individual are best served in the context of relationships rather than in isolation. Rather than prioritizing the narcissistic needs of the individual, small groups are a place where the brokenness of individuals can serve to strengthen the entire community. These groups become a place of healing, not just for the individual with the personal need but for the entire community of faith.

SALVATION FOR ME AND ME ALONE

The expression of excessive individualism in local church life is rooted in the excessive individualism of Western evangelical theology. Evangelicalism's idolatry of the individual has crippled the church's ability to view sin and salvation outside of the narrow parameters of a personal faith. Evangelical theology becomes exclusively an individual-driven theology instead of a community-driven theology. In an individual-driven theology, individual sin takes center stage. Individual sin leads to a sense of personal guilt: I, the individual, did something personally wrong and I feel guilty about my actions. I am responsible for my personal, individual actions and nothing more. Therefore, I can personally confess my sins and be absolved of my individual sinfulness and my personal feelings of guilt. Because the individual is only responsible for an individualized and personal guilt, there is no sense of shame for corporate actions that are also expressions of human sinfulness.

Our reduction of sin to a personal issue means that we are unwilling to deal with social structural evils, and this reduction prevents us from understanding the full expression of human sinfulness and fallenness. We have reduced the power of redemption to a personal salvation from personal sin. Evangelism programs and methods, such as the Four Spiritual Laws and the Bridge Illustration, focus exclusively on an individualistic worldview and emphasize a personal salvation experience.

Our approach to evangelism is shaped by an individualized soteriology (our perspective on salvation) based upon a Western framework. Our soteriology arises from our hamartiology (our understanding of the nature of sin). Our understanding of salvation is contingent upon how we understand what we are being saved from, namely sin and its consequences. When sin is limited to the individual realm and does not extend into the corporate realm, our understanding of salvation is also limited to the individual realm. Sin, therefore, is found only in the individual, not in structures and systems. The possibility of redemption, therefore, is also limited exclusively to the individual. A relationship with God limited to the private and individual realm ultimately limits our experience with God. Our understanding of sin limited to an individual level reveals a personal guilt over wrongdoing. However, lacking an understanding of corporate sin, we are unable to feel, perceive or understand the impact of the shame of corporate responsibility.

In *The Death of Satan*,[15] Andrew Delbanco laments the loss of the sense of evil in American society. Delbanco alludes to a loss of the corporate sense of evil. While not directly addressing the church, Delbanco's book is a prophetic work by a secular academic, indicting the church for our lack of understanding of the full nature and expression of sin. We are challenged as a Christian community to engage in a larger dialogue about a corporate sense of sin. Our excessive emphasis on individualism keeps us from dealing with the implication of corporate sin—it exonerates us from addressing corporate sin that may be evident in our social and political engagement. As Metzger states, "The individualistic orientation of evangelicalism structures the church and makes us blind to negative patterns of consumption and suspicious of structural engagement."[16]

Why are American evangelicals so willing to overlook corporate sin, such as the torturing of political prisoners, an unjust economic system leading to structures of poverty, or structural racism? Is it because we may personally benefit via cheaper gas prices, an improved economy and economic privilege? Is it because our favored political candidate will benefit when we overlook certain social and political injustices? As Richard Kyle explains: "Reflecting the old Puritan heritage and American individualism, evangelicals focus on abortion and sexual immorality while downplaying the issues of poverty, racism, and social injustice. And when they address such problems, they believe that they can be solved primarily through individual, church, or local efforts."[17] Corporate sin is so disconnected from the reality of our typical American Christian life that we are shocked when it actually enters our world. Rather than confront sin, we begin to look for ways to categorize it as a theologically liberal agenda—thereby stripping corporate confession and repentance of its prophetic power.

REAL EVANGELISM, NOT THAT OTHER STUFF

Furthermore, an overemphasis on individualism in our theology and practice yields an evangelical Christianity seeing social justice and racial reconciliation as a distraction from the "real work" of personal evangelism. I am often invited to speak at Christian colleges on the topic of racial reconciliation and multiethnicity. I frequently raise the theme

that being a biblical Christian community requires not just being a superficial multiethnic community where we simply tolerate one another,
but becoming a genuinely racially-reconciled community that exhibits
racial justice. I challenge the students to consider ways that systemic
and corporate racial injustice could be confronted with the gospel of
Jesus Christ. I am very hopeful at the number of positive responses from
Christian college students that reveal a deeper longing to move their
faith beyond a merely personal expression.

After one particular visit to a Christian college, I received an e-mail
from a student outlining her frustration as she attempted to raise the
issue of racial justice on her campus. "It was the theology department at
our school that shut us down. They believe that the gospel is really about
the salvation of individuals and not about a liberal, social gospel. These
justice-oriented activities distract from the real work of evangelism."
Unfortunately, this scenario has occurred enough times that it has taken
on a sense of inevitability in Christian colleges.

The concerns of many of these detractors arise from the fundamentalist-
modernist controversies of the twentieth century. Theologically conservative Christians (oftentimes referred to as fundamentalists) were at odds
with the theologically liberal Christians. Fundamentalists (and eventually their evangelical successors) held to a more theologically conservative
position, particularly related to the authority of Scripture and the person
of Jesus. Other elements began to distinguish the two groups, as liberal
Christians were seen as supporting a social gospel focusing on the redemption of society, while conservative Christians were viewed as supporting a personal evangelism focused on the individual.

Theological liberalism may be defined in the simplest terms as the acquiescence to culture by the church and the subsequent compromising of
the gospel message. Theological liberalism of the twentieth century sacrificed the high view of Scripture and an orthodox Christology for the sake
of appealing to larger cultural norms. The central criticism aimed at twentieth century theological liberals was their unwillingness to recognize the
reality of human sinfulness. This lack of recognition is attributed to theological liberalism's yielding to cultural pressures. Society didn't want to

inadequate definition; some is on track

hear about sin, so theological liberals chose to leave sin out of the discussion. Their actions reflect how theological liberals were subsumed under a Christ-*of*-culture[18] model of cultural engagement.

The tables have turned, however, since the early days of the fundamentalist-modernist controversies of the early and mid-twentieth century. The liberals of the twentieth century allowed the culture to shape their theology, but how much of American evangelicalism is now shaped by the culture? When evangelicals deny the Scriptures' call to be concerned for social justice and social concerns, we are influenced by the cultural norm of individualism, rather than Scriptural norms. What, therefore, is the real expression of liberalism in the twenty-first century?

INDIVIDUALISM AND RACE

With only an individualized theology as a reference point, American evangelicalism fails to understand the power of corporate sin, especially as it relates to racism. Racism is an individual issue that needs to be resolved by focusing on individual prejudice. But by focusing on individual prejudice, we limit the understanding of racism to strictly a personal issue. As individuals we may feel guilty about an individual act, but we do not feel the debilitating shame of the corporate sin of racism. If I merely have to confront individual prejudice, then I simply right this personal wrong (a prejudiced thought, a racial slur) by doing a positive thing to confront individual prejudice (serving at a soup kitchen, taking the Martin Luther King Jr. holiday off). I don't have to confront the shame of corporate racism, which is not so easily undone.

I was told about a panel discussion that was held on the topic of race and race relations. One of the panelists was an African American sociology professor. A well-intentioned participant spoke about his experience of working as a delivery guy in a fast-food carryout. He described how he had to deal with prejudice in his workplace among his coworkers. When a delivery request would come up from a certain Zip Code, his coworkers would remark or joke about how that particular Zip Code was a black or a Mexican neighborhood. Comments such as "be sure to take some *salsa* with you when you make the delivery to that neighborhood," or "I bet they asked for hot sauce with that order," would frequently be made. The well-intentioned young man asked how he should respond to such racism.

The professor responded: "I don't care. . . . Why are you coming to these kinds of gatherings with your trivial questions? Why aren't you concerned about the much larger and much more significant offense of why this city is segregated along racial lines according to certain Zip Codes and the subsequent economic injustice that follows?" The well-intentioned young man wanted to deal with the individual sin and ablution of guilty feelings associated with prejudice, but the professor wanted to address the systemic issues that created the deeply rooted racism that pervades our society.

When it comes to the issue of racism, it is easy to be caught up in individual slights (though they have a validity in terms of the pain caused to others), but the emphasis on individual slights has become a convenient excuse to not deal with the corporate expressions of racism. Sociologists Michael Emerson and Christian Smith point out in their landmark work *Divided by Faith*:

> Individualism is very American, but the type of individualism and the ferocity with which it is held distinguishes white evangelicals from others. . . . Contemporary white American evangelicalism is perhaps the strongest carrier of this freewill-individual tradition. The roots of this individualist tradition run deep, dating back to shortly after the sixteenth-century Reformation, extending to much of the Free Church tradition, flowering in America's frontier awakenings and revivals, and maturing in spiritual pietism and anti-Social Gospel fundamentalism.[19]

Evangelicalism's obsessive fascination with maintaining the primacy of the individual deepens the disconnect with social sin, particularly as it relates to race. "The concept of individual sin lies behind many white evangelicals' accounts of the race problem. . . . Absent from their accounts is the idea that poor relationships might be shaped by social structures, such as laws, the ways institutions operate, or forms of segregation. . . . So white evangelicals are severely constrained by their religio-cultural tools. Although much in Christian scripture and tradition points to the influence of social structures on individuals."[20]

The excessive individualism of the Western, white cultural captivity of the church reduces racism to an exclusively personal issue. Evangelicalism's captivity to excessive individualism means that outrage for the corporate sin of racism is rarely present. Satan has been able to create a social system of injustice that ultimately demeans the value and worth of the individual. We are so busy trying to justify and deny the reality of personal, individual prejudice that we ignore the larger issue of a corporate shame that arises from a structural, systemic evil. This reduction of sin to a personal, individual level ultimately hinders the fullness of the gospel message.

Consumerism and Materialism

The Soul of Western, White Cultural Captivity

A FEW YEARS AGO, I HAD THE PRIVILEGE of attending a conference focused on theology arising out of the Native American Christian context. NAIITS (the North American Institute for Indigenous Theological Studies) was one of the most stimulating and challenging conferences I have ever attended. One of the most significant challenges occurred not while listening to a plenary speaker during a main session but during a casual meal-time conversation. During dinner, I was seated next to a First Nations lay leader in his forties. During the course of our conversation he described how he had been sexually abused by the "missionary" that led the only church in the remote region. Tears and overwhelming grief came flooding out in his recounting of this tragedy. The pain was very real and it was evident that he was still struggling with these events from many years past.

As he was describing his pain and his experience, I began to think about how I would have reacted to something like that happening to me. If that had happened to me, my shadow would have never gone anywhere near the church grounds. I would have forever walked away from the church. My friend continued his story of how eventually the abuse was discovered and the cleric was removed. Upon the cleric's removal, my friend returned to that very same church. I was dumbfounded. "How could you do that?" I asked. "How could you return to the place that has caused you such pain and suffering?" He replied: "Because I love Jesus and I love his church. It was the only church in the region . . . where else would I go?"

I was deeply impressed with the level of commitment shown by this Native American believer. In contrast, I find myself operating with a completely different approach when it comes to church involvement. For example, this past Sunday our family made a nearly forty-five minute commute to our church—how many other churches did we drive by on our way to our "local" church? Why did we define "local" as a church of our choosing rather than a church of nearby location? Even after an American Christian chooses a church, he or she will entertain the prospect of leaving a church because it is not meeting his or her personal and individual needs. How easy is it for an American Christian to approach finding the right church the way we approach buying cereal at the local supermarket? We're looking for all the right ingredients and rejecting churches because they don't have our style of worship, our style of preaching, or our type of people. We're purchasing a product rather than committing to the body of Christ. We are captive to the Western, white captivity of the church in our materialistic and consumeristic bent, more accurately reflecting American culture and society than Scripture.

OUR PATRIOTIC DUTY TO SHOP

I was home with my daughter watching NBC's *Today Show.* My not-yet one-year-old was enjoying her favorite breakfast of Cheerios when the news came on over the television screen. Planes had crashed into the World Trade Center. In that moment, I knew that my daughter's world would never be the same. Everything had changed. I sensed that the security that I wanted and that I had worked so hard to attain for my family was no longer within my grasp. I wanted something that would restore order to my family's world. I needed something that would return my nation to the state of safety and worldly peace that I had come to rely upon.

Within a few weeks, a sense of peace began to be restored. I was assured that America would recover from this attack. A series of statements from the President made it clear what I needed to do to restore order to a messed-up world:

> The American economy will be open for business. . . . People need [to go about] their daily lives, working and shopping. . . . Life in America is going forward. . . . We must work together to achieve important goals for the American people here at home. This work begins with keeping our economy growing. . . . I ask your continued participation and confidence in the American economy. . . . A recent report on retail sales shows a strong beginning to the holiday shopping season across the country—and I encourage you all to go shopping more.[1]

My job as a good American was to go about my daily business and demonstrate that our way of life will persevere. I could do my part to restore order in a post-9/11 America. In the wake of the worst terrorist attack on American soil, my patriotic duty as an American was to spend money and consume consumables. To be a good shopper meant to be a good American.

Excessive materialism has the power to corrupt a society. Materialism becomes the pursuit of individual gain at the expense of what is best for society as a whole. As a result, American society becomes infected with what a PBS documentary labeled as "affluenza."

> [Affluenza is] a painful, contagious, socially transmitted condition of overload, debt, anxiety, and waste resulting form the dogged pursuit of more. . . . The affluenza epidemic is rooted in the obsessive, almost religious quest for economic expansion that has become the core principle of what is called 'the American dream.' . . . It's rooted in the idea that every generation will be materially wealthier than its predecessor, and that somehow, each of us can pursue that single-minded end without damaging the countless other things we hold dear.[2]

Our society has become infected with affluenza. Materialism and consumerism govern the way we live our lives and how we relate to each other in American society.

Materialism and consumerism reduce people to a commodity. An individual's worth in society is based upon what assets they bring and what possessions they own. The commodification of human life means that we are more than willing to terminate human life if the cost is deemed too high, whether that is the killing of an unborn child because he or she will cause undue financial strain on society or the killing of a prisoner because it costs more to keep him incarcerated. Social life is reduced to the exchange of goods and products, and human life is reduced to a consumable value based upon material worth above and beyond any spiritual worth.

Materialism also creates a sense of urgency in having our personal needs met. Because everything has a price and can be made affordable, we have been conditioned to expect quick and easy answers to problems. These answers always come in the material realm and we begin to believe that our spiritual problems can be solved with material goods. For example, scanning any bestseller list shows that the two genres that consistently outsell all others are cookbooks and diet books. These bestsellers show how self-improvement is focused upon material well-being. If you want emotional happiness, then material objects (such as food or a better body) will provide that happiness. Ultimately, affluenza atrophies the soul. "The more Americans fill their lives with things, the more they tell psychiatrists, pastors, friends, and family members that they feel 'empty' inside."[3]

GOOD AMERICAN CHRISTIANS SPEND MONEY

The Western, white captivity of the church means that the church has wholeheartedly adapted the materialistic and consumeristic worldview of American culture. To be a good American Christian means to be both a good capitalist and a good consumer within that capitalist system. "Materialism and consumerism have presented few problems for the evangelical subculture. For a long time, evangelicals have found ways to

makes me think of PMC.
Kingdom Stimulus Fund

reconcile their version of the Christian faith with the consumer-driven American culture."[4] Consumerism and capitalism have so captured American evangelicalism that, in some contexts, capitalism has become a part of evangelicalism's doctrine.

In the spring of 2007, a popular professor was fired from his position at Colorado Christian University. Professor Andrew Paquin had assigned books by Jim Wallis and Peter Singer in his classes and was perceived as unsupportive of capitalism.[5] The president of Colorado Christian University, William Armstrong, "fired Paquin from a position teaching global studies at the end of the spring semester amid concerns that his lessons were too radical and undermined the school's commitment to the free enterprise system."[6] University President Armstrong asserts that "free enterprise is fundamental to the school's philosophy. 'I don't think there is another system that is more consistent with the teachings of Jesus Christ,' Armstrong said."[7] The Western, white captivity of the church means that capitalism can be revered as the system closest to God and the consequent rampant materialism and consumerism of the capitalist system become acceptable vices.

Materialism and consumerism developed most prominently in the nineteenth century in U.S. history with the industrial revolution. "The industrial revolution produced more than the population could afford or consume. . . . A huge gap existed between production and consumption. So something had to be done. People had to be encouraged to buy more and be given the means to do so. The industrialists had to prime the pump of consumption, to increase demand to match production. They realized that they had to teach consumption as a way of life."[8] While America grappled with this growing but unrecognized problem, American Christianity, as a captive to American culture, rode the wave of increasing affluence. For "the years following World War II . . . [evangelicals] have participated in the rise of American prosperity and indulged in its consumerism."[9]

Historian George Marsden, in *Fundamentalism and American Culture*, also recognizes evangelicalism's captivity to the materialistic values of American society.

There are not many other material aspects of the American dream that most adherents are expected to give up. Rather it is usually assumed, and sometimes advertised, that the comforts of the suburbs, ability to vacation in exotic places, and economic security may well be added benefits of "seeking first the kingdom of God."[10]

American Christianity has acquiesced to the materialistic values of American society and is no longer distinguishable in its values and norms from the excessive materialism of American society.

In our everyday church life, we reflect the cultural values of materialism. For example, when we look toward the development of churches, what priorities do we have for our churches? Are we measuring success based upon Western values or scriptural values? A few years ago I was told about a church plant in a suburban community. The church had been given a fairly healthy sum to aid in its church plant. The church proceeded to use a substantial portion of those funds to pay a graphic designer to create a logo for the church. In short, a third of the church planting budget went toward a marketing effort. A few years ago, there was a popular question that made the rounds of evangelical churches— "What would Jesus do?" I wonder if Jesus would spend a third of a church planting grant to make a logo that would give the appearance of a successful church, or would those funds have been better used by serving the community?

Sometimes a Building Is Just a Building

How a church spends money oftentimes reflects the church's value system. I remember in high school visiting a church with a waterfall and a rock garden right next to the sanctuary. I could not think of a single reason why a waterfall and a rock garden were more beneficial for a church than using those funds to serve the poor in the community. I grapple with the obscene amounts of money used for church aesthetics in contrast to how churches deal with the issues of poverty and social injustice. Could hundreds of thousands of dollars spent on improving a

He seems to have a problem with aesthetics but then felon he takes on dying small style churches.

church's aesthetics be better used by funneling funds to express compassion and concern for the poor?

In the last twenty-five years, there have been two dominant forms of
church architecture: the movie theater and the mall, oftentimes with the
two forms going hand in hand. In many sanctuaries, the seats are ar-
ranged in an amphitheater style with comfortable stadium seating that
mirrors movie-theater seating, along with a large projection screen at
the front of the auditorium. Ushers work diligently to seat the viewers in
their plush and comfortable seats. Furthermore, in the design of the
church as a whole, the shopping mall becomes the architectural
inspiration.

Some sociologists have noted that malls are increasingly taking the
place of churches as a gathering place for ceremonial community life.
Malls have a "similarity to the religious, ceremonial centers of traditional civilizations of the ancient world."[11] Items found in the center of
malls, such as a fountain or a large tree, reflect religious symbolism. The
mall becomes the center for social life as "communities, large and small,
and within their various quarters and sections, are being reorganized
around or in relation to various types of shopping malls . . . The mall is
the new village square, encompassing all the social and economic forces
associated with that expression of human community."[12] The role of the
mall is to create a cultic symbol and create a sense of worship at the altar
of materialism and consumerism.

The American evangelical church has returned the favor by building
church buildings that take on both the form and function of a shopping
mall. I was visiting a megachurch in the South. When I entered the
foyer, I was greeted by a long hallway with various options. There was a
bookstore, a coffee shop, a place where church T-shirts and parapherna-
lia were being sold, a store where I could buy Christian music CDs and
sermon CDs, and a playground reminiscent of any McDonald's playland
in America. The entrance to the sanctuary was a nondescript set of
doors. If someone had blindfolded me and put me in the lobby, I would
have had a difficult time discerning that I was in a church, rather than
a shopping mall. Our movie-theater sanctuaries (to appease the con-

sumer looking for an hour's worth of entertainment on a Sunday morning) and our mall-like church buildings reveal our captivity to the materialistic and consumeristic culture of American society.

I address the topic of materialism expressed in our church buildings because I have seen local congregations struggle mightily with this issue. I have seen numerous examples of material and consumer excesses expressed through the venue of the church building. I have also seen churches try to emerge out of the cultural value of materialism to use their buildings to greatly benefit God's kingdom. When I was a church planter in Cambridge, it was a Nazarene congregation that opened their building to not only our church but to many other churches and community events. The Nazarene church received minimal financial benefit from sharing their space with us, but our two congregations worked together to serve and reach our immediate neighborhood. A church in Chicago embarked on a building campaign, not for the typical reason of improving the aesthetics of the building for their own enjoyment, but in order to create more space for neighborhood outreach programs. I know of two different churches in California that have delayed building projects in order to sustain and increase their mission giving. These churches may not have the material expression of a beautiful building, but their choices have served the work of God's kingdom.

In the summer of 2008, at the Evangelical Covenant Church denominational annual meeting, I witnessed the power of a church freed from the cultural captivity of materialism. Crown Valley Covenant Church believed that they had run the final lap of the race. Their diminishing membership was exhausted. Yet, they wanted to honor Jesus, even as they were drawing their last breath as a church in their community. So the church turned over twelve million dollars of assets to the church planting fund of the denomination. Those funds would be used to help plant forty new churches—many of them would be immigrant, ethnic minority and multiethnic churches. As the seed of this white church died and was buried, it proceeded to produce a crop fortyfold.

The church had the option of hanging on for dear life. The church could have sold off their assets a little bit at a time until the membership was depleted. They could have even chosen to sell the assets and divide the proceeds among the remaining members of the church. But they chose not to lay claim to material possessions and yielded their wealth to further kingdom work. This act of humility by Crown Valley Covenant Church was a casting off of the cloak of materialism. A material-focused worldview would have demanded that Crown Valley hang on to their resources to the bitter end. But instead, they chose to invest in the next evangelicalism.

THE TRAPPINGS OF MATERIALISM

Materialism, however, is not limited to what we physically own as churches (such as our buildings), but also extends to our mindset and approach to church life. Because of our materialistic bent and our consumer mentality, our spirituality can become shallow. When life is reduced to a materialistic exchange of goods, our spiritual life can also be reduced to an exchange of goods. Spiritual life becomes a consumable product that is exchanged only if it benefits the material and corporal well-being of the individual consumer. We begin to think of ourselves as consumers when we relate to our local church.

For example, at a church leadership meeting, in response to a specific question by "Jack," I stated (rather flippantly and probably less pastorally than I should have), "This church does not exist to make Jack happy." To which Jack replied: "Actually, I think this church does exist to make me happy." The implication being, if the church does not make me happy, it is very easy for me to find another church that will strive to make me happy.

One of my friends who pastors a fairly large and affluent white church invited an African American academic to preach on the issue of racial reconciliation at a Sunday service. The invited guest spoke passionately and strongly about the biblical need for racial justice and the socio-historical need for reconciliation. That evening and the following day, the pastor received numerous e-mails expressing anger that the topic had been approached in the manner that it was. Most of the e-mails questioned why the speaker had been invited to their church. One particular e-mail asked the pastor to guarantee that he would never have to feel that uncomfortable in a church setting again. If that guarantee was not forthcoming, then there were plenty of options to attend a different church where he would not be challenged to confront racial injustice.

American evangelicalism has created the unique phenomenon of church shopping—viewing church as yet another commodity and product to be evaluated and purchased. When a Christian family moves to a new city, how much of the standards by which they choose a church is based upon a shopping list of their personal tastes and wants rather than their commitment to a particular community or their desire to serve a particular neighborhood? Churches, in turn, have adapted their ministries to appeal to the consumer mindset of the American public. As Metzger asserts, "Many evangelical church leaders believe that the best way to multiply churches quickly is to make the members feel comfortable rather than comfort them with the cross that breaks down the divisions between God, us, and others."[13]

The acquiescence to consumer culture means that churches fall into the vicious cycle of trying to keep the attendees happy. When a church entices consumers by using marketing techniques and materialistic considerations, is it possible to change that approach after the individual begins attending the church? Or has it set up the church in such a way that the church attendee expects the same level of accommodation that was available when they were church shopping? Can a relationship that began on the level of an exchange of goods and services transition to a deeper level of commitment? Even when the church seeks to develop a small group ministry that would deepen the member's involvement, the establishing of that small group community falls along certain lines of affinity, so that now the church consumer is shopping for a small group that meets his or her criteria or personal preferences. Breaking through a consumer mindset that is dominant in the culture and has found its way into the church becomes more and more difficult. Materialism and consumerism become the enticement into the church but also become the trap of maintaining and growing the church.

MEASURING SUCCESS

Over the last decade or so, I have had the opportunity to travel to different cities throughout the United States on various preaching and teaching engagements. My travels allow me the opportunity to see the wide range of expressions found in the evangelical church in different regions of America. I make it a point to ask someone from the host church or institution to tell me about the successful churches in the area. Without fail, I will be directed toward the church with the largest attendance in the region. A typical answer will be: "You've got to visit _____ Church. They draw over ten thousand worshipers."

How do we measure "success" in the typical American church—by the standards of Scripture or by the standards of the American consumer value system? Typically, we will see the success of churches measured by the numerical size of the church and the financial health of the church (oftentimes reflected in the condition and appearance of the church building). In more colloquial language, we focus on the ABCs of church success: Attendance, Buildings and Cash. Or even more directly, the three Bs of church success: Building, Bucks and Butts. The church holds the same materialistic values held by American society. We measure success in the church with standards as worldly as the most secular Fortune 500 company. Churches are no more than businesses (albeit nonprofit ones) with the bottom line being the number of attendees or the size of the church budget. American evangelicalism is held captive to the materialistic and consumeristic values of American society.

When we measure success by Western values, we create heroes out of those who succeed by Western culture's standards over and above the standards of Scripture. The pastor that fulfills an American definition of success becomes a leader in the evangelical community. If you pastor a megachurch or have authored a *New York Times* bestseller, then you now have the capacity and wisdom to save entire nations and continents. If you are successful in the United States in developing and marketing your church, then your ideas are applicable in nearly every setting. If you can make it here, then you'll make it anywhere.

Material success in the United States means that your systems, ideas and values can be duplicated and transmitted to a poor, starving, war-torn nation with the same level of material success. Material success in the West means that you will make the cover of a major Christian publication, a white face surrounded by the faces of happy black kids because you have come to save their continent. Material success in the West means that your bestseller author status gives you the ability to know what's best for the complexities of confronting poverty in a foreign country.

The *Wall Street Journal* reported the story of Bruce Wilkinson, who had authored a *New York Times* bestseller called *The Prayer of Jabez.* "In 2002 Bruce Wilkinson, a Georgia preacher whose self-help prayer book had made him a rich man, heard God's call, moved to Africa and announced his intention to save one million children left orphaned by the AIDS epidemic."[14] Wilkinson's motivation and intentions were unquestionably noble. However, coming from a materialistic worldview, Western standards formed his view of success in his dreams for Africa. Wilkinson proposed a $190 million project called the "African Dream Village" to be built in Swaziland.

It would provide homes for ten thousand orphans. Each home would have a bed-and-breakfast suite where tourists would pay $500 a week to stay, combining charity with an African vacation. Fifty such homes would form a mini village of a thousand orphans, built around a theme—such as Wild West rodeos or Swazi village life—to entertain guests. There would also be a new luxury hotel and an 18-hole golf course. Orphans would be trained as rodeo stars and safari guides at nearby game reserves. The idea, Mr. Wilkinson said, was to "try to bring experiences to the kids they could only get at Walt Disney or a dude ranch."[15]

Wilkinson's demands to the Swazi government for a ninety-nine-year lease for prime real estate were rebuffed. "In October [2005], Mr. Wilkinson resigned in a huff from the African charity he founded. He abandoned his plan to house 10,000 children in a facility that was to be an orphanage, bed-and-breakfast, game reserve, Bible college, industrial park and Disneyesque tourist destination in the tiny kingdom of Swaziland."[16] Wilkinson's success in American publishing did not translate into success in Africa.

Our Western, white cultural captivity allows us to lift up Western values and norms of success in our churches and in our leaders—leading to a paternalistic attitude in how we duplicate and multiply Western, white models in non-Western cultures and systems. Material success in the West generates heroes who are out to solve all of the world's problems with a five-step plan. Usually this approach results in the perception that the rich white male has all the right answers for the poor blacks. Is it possible to overcome Western, white cultural captivity and pursue a biblical model of economic justice?

LET JUSTICE ROLL DOWN

In our pursuit of success based upon material norms, have we become more and more unwilling to confront sin? For example, would we be more willing to confront environmental injustice if we didn't benefit economically from the abuse of the natural world? Have we sold our souls to be relevant? How substantially different would the church look if we measured success on the basis of the parable of the sheep and the goats of Matthew 25 or the self-sacrificial community of Acts 2 instead of measuring success based upon cultural values of consumerism and materialism? The American evangelical church needs to break the shackles of consumerism and materialism and turn instead toward biblical values in understanding and measuring success.

The prophet Amos confronted Israel during a time of relative peace and prosperity. Israel was experiencing a time of political and military stability leading to tremendous economic prosperity. As a result of this stability and prosperity, there was in Israel the creation of excess wealth leading to a leisured upper class.[17] Consequently, a sharp division had developed between upper and lower classes, between the landowners and peasants. The upper class of Israel's society was living a life of decadence, luxury and self-indulgence[18] characterized by winter houses, summer houses, and houses and mansions adorned with ivory (Amos 3:15), with "beds inlaid with ivory" (Amos 6:4), and drinking "wine by the bowlful" (Amos 6:6). This lifestyle of excessive materialism indicated a deeper, underlying social and spiritual decay. Economic injustice was rampant, where "they sell the innocent for silver, and the needy for a pair of sandals. They trample on the heads of the poor . . . and deny justice to the oppressed" (Amos 2:6-7). They "oppress the poor and crush the needy" (Amos 4:1) while they "deprive the poor of justice in the courts" (Amos 5:12). "The state of Israel, externally strong, prosperous, and confident of the future, was inwardly rotten and sick past curing."[19]

The combination of affluence and spiritual decay led Israel to seek to replace their spiritual emptiness with only the externalities of worship life. The people of Israel during the time of Amos were polished worshipers. A religious festival during this time used the best of all possible material goods to make it the best festival ever. Similar to the successful American evangelical churches of the late twentieth and early twenty-first centuries, they worshiped in the best building, used the best materials, hired the best musicians, and exhibited top-notch professionalism in their worship life. The modern equivalent would be a state-of-the-art building made out of the finest materials, using the most high-tech media equipment, with professional musicians and speakers leading a highly polished service. The nation of Israel had replaced an internal depth of true spiritual worship with the external superficialities of professional worship.

The twin towers of affluence and festival life led Israel to believe that they were impervious to judgment. If YHWH were to judge, surely he would judge those evil pagan nations that bordered Israel. Israel was so certain that they were exempt from judgment and that they would, in fact, receive additional blessings that they were eagerly anticipating the day of the Lord (Amos 5:18). In biblical literature, the day of the Lord was the appointed day when YHWH would come to wipe out all of his enemies. Israel believed that the day of the Lord would be a day of more affluence and prosperity—after all, wasn't their material prosperity and their vibrant worship life veritable proof of their blessed status? There was an illusion and a dream of where their life was headed.

I grew up in a Korean immigrant church. Part of the sociological function of the immigrant church is to help in the process of assimilation to larger, mainstream society. The immigrant church may be involved in that process in either a positive or a destructive way. A dysfunctional expression of this process in the Asian American immigrant church context is the confusion between the American dream and the will of God. In an attempt to better assimilate into American society, immigrant communities will often co-opt the existing narrative of the host culture. The dominant culture's values become the values that many immigrant groups try to emulate. Being a good Christian in America means being a good American Christian. Therefore, the value of pursuing a materialistic vision of one's life gets confused with a vision of a healthy and mature spiritual life.

Instead of providing a spiritual and theological corrective to the materialistic narrative of American culture, my particular immigrant church chose to embrace the message of material success. The message for the children of immigrants becomes:

> If you want to be a good Christian and a good American, then you need to get good grades in high school, become active in clubs and student government. As a result you will get into a good college. When you get into that good college, get good grades and become active in the clubs, so that you can get into the right graduate school (law school or medical school or a master's program in engineering). Graduate and get a good-paying job. Marry a nice Christian spouse with the same values. Buy a nice four-bedroom suburban home in a "safe neighborhood." Make sure the house has a two-car garage to house a Japanese import for your everyday commute and a German import for your Sunday drive to church. All along be involved in your church just enough to remember your Christian heritage. Have good kids who will in turn go to good schools so that the cycle can begin all over again. After the cycle has run its course, do everything possible to preserve the security you have established so that the next generation will have

the opportunity to pursue the same success as the previous generation.

Even as Christians pursue this dream, there is an assumption that they are doing the godly thing. The American dream becomes confused with biblical standards. As more and more wealth and possessions are accumulated by the Christian, there is an assumption that they are in the will of God and that more blessings are coming their way.

In the book of Amos, we see that the people of Israel had deluded themselves into believing that their material prosperity and their superficial worship merited further blessing. But instead of a blessing, YHWH brings a curse. Instead of "Blessed are you," Amos cries out "Woe." "Woe to you who long for the day of the LORD" (Amos 5:18). "Woe to you who are complacent in Zion, and to you who feel secure on Mount Samaria" (Amos 6:1). The curse of God falls upon Israel, seemingly unexpectedly and surprisingly. In the same way, are we assuming that our material success obligates God to continue to provide material blessings? We are shocked when the privilege of wealth goes unrecognized by God, and instead of God's delight in our worship, we find God's unexpected but righteous judgment.

The New Testament passage with a parallel theme to Amos 5 may be found in Matthew 25. Matthew 25 provides a vivid picture of the Judgment Day. In this passage, Jesus comes to judge the earth and divides humanity into the sheep and the goats. The judgment that falls upon the goats is unexpected, as the goats cannot believe that their inaction toward the poor merits God's judgment. The goats are expecting the praise of God for their other accomplishments. They can refer to a long list of material accomplishments for their church. They have built the beautiful buildings, established the successful churches and delighted in material blessings. Why then, are the goats being cast into the lake of fire? Because they have relied upon their economic and material prosperity to measure their successes rather than recognizing that what they've done and not done to the very least of their brothers and sisters is the true measure of success.

SHORT-TERM VS. LONG-TERM GAIN

In the pursuit of the short-term benefit of material gain, the church has sacrificed the long-term benefits of being the kingdom of God, the body of Christ and the bride of Jesus. We have fulfilled the words of Scripture by selling the church's long-term well-being for the sake of a short-term prosperity. "What good is it for you to gain the whole world, yet forfeit your soul" (Mk 8:36). One of the central characteristics of a materialistic worldview is to seek short-term solutions despite long-term negative consequences. When meeting the materialistic needs of the individual becomes the central expression of the church, there will be short-term productivity but with negative long-term consequences. "North American Christianity has difficulty understanding and living out the gospel because the church has become all too captive to a consumerist mindset that focuses attention on meeting needs, on personal growth, and on personal choice."[20] We as the church have sold our souls to gain the material affluence of the world.

As Metzger writes, "Jesus needs to cleanse the temple again today; he needs to overturn the tables of commerce and consumption, for consumer Christianity continues to turn the temple into a market. Greedy zeal for a false utopian vision of homogeneity and upward mobility threatens to consume the church, rebuilding the wall of division between those of different ethnicities and classes through free market consumer church-growth strategies, as well as prosperity-gospel preaching to the poor."[21] Our short-term desire to keep our church attendees happy has led to an effective ministry that serves white, middle-class suburbanites[22] but has essentially become irrelevant in proclaiming and demonstrating the kingdom principles of peace and justice.

Is it possible to break the captivity of the evangelical church to the trap of materialism and consumerism? Recently, Willow Creek Community Church examined their ministry practices over the course of the last few decades. Arguably, Willow Creek has been one of the most influential churches in the latter half of the twentieth century—oftentimes cited for its incorporation of business practices and the measuring of success using largely materialistic and consumeristic means. As the

Chicago Tribune recently reported, "For more than three decades, Willow Creek Community Church has defined its success by tallying the throngs who walk through its doors."[23] The recently released report

> reveals that most of what they have been doing for these many years and what they have taught millions of others to do is not producing solid disciples of Jesus Christ. Numbers yes, but not disciples . . . Hybels laments: *Some of the stuff that we have put millions of dollars into thinking it would really help our people grow and develop spiritually, when the data actually came back it wasn't helping people that much. Other things that we didn't put that much money into and didn't put much staff against is stuff our people are crying out for.* . . . The one individual who has had perhaps the greatest influence on the American church in our generation has now admitted his philosophy of ministry, in large part, was a "mistake."[24]

The succeeding generation of churches has begun to recognize that an affluenza and market-driven church that appeals to the materialistic desires of the individual consumer has resulted in a comfortable church, but not a biblical church. The church's captivity to materialism has resulted in the unwillingness to confront sins such as economic and racial injustice and has produced consumers of religions rather than followers of Jesus. But can the American church recognize her captivity to the materialistic values of American culture and return to the biblical call to justice as we move toward the next evangelicalism?

3

Racism

The Residue of Western, White Cultural Captivity

IT WAS A TYPICAL TUESDAY-MORNING STAFF MEETING at our church. We were taking our first coffee break when I decided to go over the week's mail. In one of the many church supply catalogs we receive, I stumbled across a full-page advertisement for Vacation Bible School curriculum from a major denomination's publishing arm. Initially I thought that the advertisement was a spoof, some sort of joke—I didn't want to believe that this was a real advertisement for actual Vacation Bible School material. The ad showed a white girl dressed in a kimono with chopsticks in her hair. She held a Chinese takeout food box. The title of this VBS material was "Rickshaw Rally: Far Out, Far East." When I typed in the website address for the curriculum, a gong appeared with (for lack of a better term) "ching-chongy" music in the background. Under the auspices of doing a VBS with a Japanese theme, the publisher caricatured and generalized all Asian cultures with various stereotypical images.[1]

Many who saw the material expressed concern ranging from the insensitive and stereotypical portrayal of Asians to the absence of input from the Asian American community in the creation of this VBS material. I personally received a large number of e-mails from Asian American Christians expressing pain and outrage over the content of the material. When a significant number of Asian American pastors and Christians went to the publisher to protest the material, our concerns were dismissed. Rather than listen and learn from the outcry of a wide range of voices, including many from within its denomination, the publisher chose to ignore these concerns.[2] So despite the breadth of the criticism and objection, the curriculum went forward with minimal cosmetic changes—particularly when it came to many of the kitschy items available for purchase, such as the karate-kid key chain and the name tags in the shape of Chinese takeout food boxes.

What still affects me to this day is how this Christian company handled the situation. The arrogant and privileged position that would not allow for repentance and retribution by the guilty party reveals an unwillingness to deal with the sin of racism in any real way. The initial slight of creating this racially offensive material was amplified by the white leadership of this denomination and their publishing arm in their insensitive and intransigent response. The entire conflict over the Rickshaw Rally VBS curriculum taught me a lesson regarding the state of race relations in the evangelical church: we still have a very long way to go. In addition, it became evident that there is an unwillingness to deal with the issue of race. It was easier to deny the sin than to confront it and transform the system that created the commission of the sin of racism. While racial issues create an emotional tension and angst, the white captivity of the church means that we lack the tools to deal with racism in a constructive and productive way.

THE CONSTRUCT OF THE RACE MYTH

The category of race has no scientific justification. As a person of Korean ancestry, I have as much in common genetically and biologically with a Swede, a Zulu or a Lakota as I do with someone of Chinese ancestry. While different theories abound regarding the origins of the category of race, it is largely acknowledged that race is a sociologically created category, rather than a scientifically created one. "Races are not biologically differentiated groupings but rather social construction."[3]

"Many scientist are now declaring that the concept of race has no basis in the biological sciences; more and more are concurring that race should be seen as a social invention."[4] It is also clear that the category of race as applied in American society does not exist in the Bible.

The Bible refers to people groups and nations, but does not distinguish people groups based upon skin color. The Bible's use of the term *people groups* does not presume race (as we use the term in the West) as a means of distinction and differentiation before YHWH. J. Daniel Hays, in *From Every People and Nation,* states "that the basic common denominator of ethnic identity, that which shows up most frequently, is that of territory and common myth of descent."[5] Race serves as a central identifier in contemporary American society, focusing on skin color and other physical characteristics. In Scripture, ethnicity based upon language, culture, social boundaries, and geographic location becomes the method of distinction.[6] Another example of Scripture's use of people groups and ethnicity rather than race as the main point of distinction can be found by looking through basic Bible dictionaries and encyclopedias. In the *International Standard Bible Encyclopedia,* the only entry for *race* reads "See Table of Nations." In the *New Bible Dictionary,* there is no entry for *race.* The biblical terminology does not include the defining of people simply by their racial characteristics.

The category of race was created by American society in an attempt to justify and regulate the social injustice of slavery. Initially, slavery in the American colonies involved both blacks and whites and did not involve hereditary slavery. "African American laborers during the first four decades after their arrival, that is, up until 1660, were not lifetime hereditary bondmen and bondwomen; rather, their status was essentially the same as that of European-American bond-laborers, namely limited-term bond-servitude."[7] The distinction of black slaves and white indentured servants needed categories of racial difference—whether by common sense, by "scientific" rationalization or by legal fiat. "In 1640 three servants, one of them a black man named John Punch, escaped from their duties in Virginia. When they were apprehended, the white servants were punished by having time added to their period of service.

Punch, on the other hand, was sentenced to service for the rest of his life."[8] The creation of the category of race allowed one group of people (self-identified as white) to enslave another group of people (designated as black).

Racial distinctions based upon measurable physical distinctions were hard to justify but it became necessary to uphold the unjust system of slavery. "A 'black' was a lifelong slave, unworthy of political enfranchisement, and denied legal protection from abuse. 'Black' symbolized savagery, ignorance, lack of intelligence, and an inability to live in a civilized manner. . . . Color categories were correlated with cultural meaning. 'Whites' were viewed as civilized, intelligent, capable of self-government, and self restraint."[9] The codification and establishment of race became a means of social control. Ivan Hannaford, in *Race: the History of an Idea in the West,* speaks of the invention of race:

> It was not until after the French and American Revolutions and the social upheavals which followed that the idea of race was fully conceptualized and became deeply embedded in our understandings and explanations of the world. In other words, the dispositions and presuppositions of race and ethnicity were introduced—some would say "invented" or "fabricated"—in modern times.[10]

The category of race is a product of Western social history.

In early American legal history, the defining of race vacillated between using the common knowledge approach and the scientific evidence approach. "Under a common knowledge approach, courts justified the assignment of petitioners to one race or another by reference to common beliefs about race."[11] The use of the common knowledge approach signified the belief that the category of race was determined by the values and norms of society. The scientific evidence approach claimed that there were scientific reasons for racial distinctions. The use of both approaches in legal cases reflected a belief that both social norms and scientific evidence shape the definition of race. However, legal proceedings began to reject the scientific evidence approach.

The courts deciding racial prerequisite cases initially relied on both rationales to justify their decisions. However, beginning in 1909 a schism appeared among the courts over whether common knowledge or scientific evidence was the appropriate standard. . . . The early congruence of and subsequent contradiction between common knowledge and scientific evidence set the terms of a debate about whether race is a social construction or a natural occurrence. In these terms, the Supreme Court's elevation of common knowledge as the legal meter of race convincingly demonstrates that racial categorization finds its origins in social practices.[12]

Because the category of race had no scientific justification, the determination of racial categories became dependent on legal cases that relied upon social norms for its definition. As Lopez concludes: "That common knowledge emerged as the only workable racial test shows that race is something which must be measured in terms of what people believe, that it is a socially mediated idea. The social construction of the White race is manifest in the Court's repudiation of science and its installation of common knowledge as the appropriate racial meter of Whiteness."[13]

The problem of defining race is an example of a vicious circle. Racism created the categories of race (commonly-held, social perceptions of physical differences); and in turn, racial distinctions became codified legally, leading to further expressions of racism in individual, social, political and legal forms. The American creation of race as a social category ultimately had a negative social impact. If the category of race was created under the auspices of equality and affirmation of difference, the outcome may have been different. However, the creation of race as a social category had dysfunctional and sinful origins. This original sinfulness has crept into our society and culture and begins to determine how we value the "norm" in American society (and subsequently the American church). Racism, therefore, ends up creating social values and norms that become the way our culture conducts business. Racism is America's original and most deeply rooted sin.

AMERICA'S ORIGINAL SIN

As an evangelism professor, one of the expectations of my job is to teach seminary students how to lead an individual to Christ. I consider this task to be a critical part of theological education. In the process of leading a person to Christ, I do not suggest that we ask an individual to recount every single sin that he or she has ever committed. A process like that would take too long and maybe the person would lose interest after the first three days. But rather, in leading a person to Christ, I need to get to the heart of the matter by dealing with the power of original sin and the process of breaking its power with the power of the blood of Jesus.

In the same way, when we deal with the corporate sin of America, do we deal with every specific sin ever committed by American society, culture and politics, or do we address the power of America's original sin? We are quick to deal with the symptoms of sin in America, but oftentimes are unwilling to deal with the original sin of America: namely, the kidnapping of Africans to use as slave labor, and usurping of lands belonging to Native Americans and subsequent genocide of indigenous peoples. As John Dawson asserts in *Healing America's Wounds*, "We have our own unfinished business, particularly with Native Americans and Afro-Americans."[14] Dawson goes on to outline the various ways in U.S. history in which injustices were committed: the violation of treaties with Native Americans, the enslavement of Africans in the New World and the abusive handling of Chinese labor in California and the West.[15] These corporate sins have left their spiritual mark on America. This original sin of racism has had significant and ongoing social and corporate implications for the church in America.

All humanity is tainted with the blight of sin and the proclivity toward sinfulness. In the same way, various cultures and people groups reflect symptoms of a fallen humanity. Throughout history, this human sinfulness has manifested itself in different ways in different cultures, oftentimes as destructive behavior toward other people groups. The specific expression of corporate sinfulness in American society seems to be in the creation of racial categories in order to further exploitation and oppression of one group over another.

When we use the term *racism,* we often see this only in individual terms. As a consequence, there is often a strong, visceral and vehement denial: "I am not a racist! I have never personally owned a slave and I have never personally taken land away from a Native American, therefore, I cannot be a racist." These types of statements reduce racism purely to individual actions and behavior. If we use the language of individual sin to address sin, then no individual is guilty. We may have our prejudices, but no individual in twenty-first-century America has actually owned a slave or taken land away from a Native American. It is too easy to dismiss and disavow individual culpability for the sin of racism. But if we use the language of corporate sin, then we are all complicit. Anyone that has benefited from America's original sin is guilty of that sin and bears the corporate shame of that sin.

I was speaking at a gathering of Asian American Christian college students at a prestigious Ivy League institution. I was covering the topic of racial and economic justice with a group of extremely bright individuals who were beneficiaries of the best education that America could offer. As I spoke on the issue of a historical economic injustice perpetrated against African Americans and Native Americans, I began to sense the potential response of these Asian American college students. "This issue doesn't apply to me. Sure, horrible atrocities have been committed against African Americans and Native Americans—but that was a long time ago. Asian Americans didn't arrive in the U.S. in any significant numbers until after 1965. Surely, we are not guilty of these injustices?"

In anticipation of this response, I addressed the corporate responsibility of American society. I spoke to these Ivy League college students and reminded them they were sitting in a building on land that had once been owned by Native Americans, and they were in a school whose robust endowment could be attributed to a successful economy that had been built on slave labor. While they may not have individually committed a personal sin against these communities, they had certainly benefitted from these past atrocities.

When we claim that we are not complicit in the corporate sin of racism, we fail to grasp how being a beneficiary of an unjust system yields a culpability for those that benefit from that system. As an example, imagine that you were starting a new business. If someone were to come to you and offer a building lease for no cost and promise to provide labor at no cost, you would have to be the worst business person in human history to fail at that business. Economic success can be assumed when you have been given free land and free labor. The American economy was built upon free land stolen from the Native American community and free labor kidnapped from Africa. Our current economic success owes a large debt to an initial economic foundation built upon free land and free labor. If we live as financial beneficiaries in the twenty-first century of this system of injustice, we have a corporate culpability and responsibility, even as we claim innocence in our personal, individual lives.

John Dawson challenges us to deal with our corporate sins by stating:

> If we have broken our covenants with God and violated our rela-
> tionships with one another, the path to reconciliation must begin
> with the act of confession. The greatest wounds in human history,
> the greatest injustices, have not happened through the acts of
> some individual perpetrator, rather through the institutions, sys-
> tems, philosophies, cultures, religions and governments of man-
> kind. Because of this, we as individuals, are tempted to absolve
> ourselves of all individual responsibility. Unless somebody identi-
> fies themselves with corporate entities, such as the nation of our
> citizenship, or the subculture of our ancestors, the act of honest
> confession will never take place. This leaves us in a world of injury
> and offense in which no corporate sin is ever acknowledged, rec-
> onciliation never begins and old hatreds deepen.[16]

Our corporate sin of racism and our corporate life as beneficiaries of a racist system require our corporate confession. This corporate confession must be led by those with a spiritual understanding and a biblical conviction—namely, the body of Christ in America.

WHITE PRIVILEGE
Acknowledging the corporate responsibility and culpability of the sin of

racism can lead to the revelation of the system of white privilege, a system that oftentimes goes unrecognized in the dialogue on race. The explicit expression of the sin of racism is still evident in American society, but it has also taken a more subtle form in the expression of white privilege. "White privilege is the other side of racism."[17] White privilege is the system that places white culture in American society at the center with all other cultures on the fringes. "Research—into books, museums, the press, advertising, films, television, software—repeatedly shows that in Western representation whites are overwhelmingly and disproportionately predominant, have the central and elaborated roles, and above all are placed as the norm, the ordinary, the standard."[18]

While North America is becoming more and more multiethnic and we are seeing more nonwhite cultural expressions, white culture remains as the primary standard by which all other cultures are judged. An unfair advantage and privilege, therefore, is given to whites in a society that reveres and prioritizes them. "The equation of being white with being human secures a position of power. White people have power and believe that they think, feel and act like and for all people; white people, unable to see their particularity, cannot take account of other people's; white people create the dominant images of the world and don't quite see that they thus construct the world in their own image; white people set standards for humanity by which they are bound to succeed and others bound to fail."[19] Latino American theologian Virgilio Elizondo speaks of the ongoing nature of white privilege by stating: "It is the dominant society that sets the norms and projects the image of success, achievement, acceptability, normalcy, and status. It is the dominant group that sets up the educational process that passes on the traditions and values of the dominant society."[20]

Privilege, therefore, is power. Privilege, when it is unnamed, holds an even greater power. It is the invisible knapsack (as Peggy McIntosh names it)[21] that gives a position of privilege based upon racial characteristics. The power of privilege is that it can go undetected by those who are oppressed by it and even by those who have it. "It has allowed some white people to create a world in their own image and a system of values that reinforces the power and privilege of those who are white people. At the same time, because of its invisibility, it has helped foster that those who succeed do so because of their superior intelligence, their hard work or their drive, rather than, at least in part, their privilege."[22] White privilege not only deals with an economic benefit, but also speaks to a position of emotional and social power that is oftentimes reserved for white Americans.

WHO DEFINES AMERICA?

One of the key political issues in the first decade of the twenty-first century is the issue of immigration. In the 2008 presidential race, the issue of immigration spurred passionate debate. Harsh rhetoric and generalizations were used in the immigration debate, evoking inflammatory terminology that spoke to the racial identity of the United States. The candidate considered the most evangelical was also the candidate that evoked the harshest rhetoric against immigration. Immigration became a hot-button political issue.

I was at a consultation in Washington, D.C., exploring the need for comprehensive immigration reform. One of the participants was an aide to a senator who was supportive of a compassionate immigration policy. She stated that, after the senator had proposed the bill, their office began to receive thousands of bricks (either as a threat or to help build a wall at the Mexican border)—enough bricks for the mailroom attendant to make a barbeque grill in his backyard. Incoming mail ran four hundred to one opposing immigration reform, oftentimes proposing nearly draconian measures to stem the tide of immigration.

In 2004 Harvard professor Samuel Huntington wrote in *Who Are We?* that the United States' racial identity needed to remain white, Anglo and Protestant. Huntington is troubled by the changing demographics of American society. "The ideologies of multiculturalism and diversity eroded the legitimacy of the remaining central elements of American identity, the cultural core and the American Creed. . . . America's third major wave of immigration that began in the 1960's brought to America people primarily from Latin America and Asia rather than Europe as the previous wave did. The culture and values of their countries of origin often differ substantially from those prevalent in America."[23] Huntington's concern is that "the elimination of the racial and ethnic components of national identity and the challenges to its cultural and creedal components raise questions concerning the prospects for American identity."[24] In other words, the more non-European immigrants come to the United States, the less American this nation becomes.

Huntington believes that more than an ideology or creed is needed in order to unify a nation. "Globalization, multiculturalism, cosmopolitanism, immigration, subnationalism, and anti-nationalism has battered American consciousness. Ethnic, racial, and gender identities came to the fore. In contrast to their predecessors, many immigrants were ampersands, maintaining dual loyalties and dual citizenships. A massive Hispanic influx raised questions concerning America's linguistic and cultural unity."[25]

As the demographics of American culture began to change, the reaction from some academics and politicians was to support an American society rooted in white America. Opponents of immigration reform (among whom are a significant number of evangelicals) are raising the question, Who gets to define what America looks like in the twenty-first century? Should every effort be made to maintain a white majority that reflects the current Western European culture and ethos of American society?

The unavoidable reality is that, by the year 2050, projections point to a nation without an ethnic majority. America will no longer be a Euro-centric, white nation. Furthermore, as previously stated, the nonwhite population among Christians is growing at a rate faster than the general population. American Christianity will become nonwhite before the rest of American society. Even now, most denominations are faced with the reality that unless they see growth among the ethnic minority population within their denomination, they will experience steady decline.

The question of immigration presents an interesting dilemma for majority-culture Christians. Immigrants and ethnic minorities are saving American Christianity. Immigrants and ethnic minorities tend to be socially and morally conservative. (If the religious right were committed to overturning *Roe v. Wade,* there is an easy solution. Give citizenship to the twelve million undocumented aliens, who are largely politically conservative and would turn the tide and momentum of the abortion debate.) Immigrant and ethnic minority churches are restoring spiritual vitality and fervor oftentimes missing in many white evangelical churches. Too often, the future of American evangelicalism is viewed as a battle over the heart and soul of middle America (i.e., white America), when the restoration of faith in American culture may actually depend on the ongoing growth of immigrant and ethnic minority Christian communities.

So what is the response of the white evangelical community to the changing face of America? So far, it has been one of conspicuous silence on the issue of immigration. Many Christian leaders have been hesitant to support genuine immigration reform—possibly reflecting the fear of a nonwhite America and a nonwhite American Christianity.

Evangelicals claim Scripture as having primary authority in a believer's life and conduct. What then, is the biblical response to the issue of immigration? In my study of Scripture, I have yet to find a single passage which supports the right to bear arms. (I'm not arguing against the right to bear arms, I'm just saying I can't find a biblical reference regarding the right to bear arms.) I have, however, found numerous references (close to one hundred) calling believers to care for the alien among them. Why is it, then, that I am more likely to find members of the National Rifle Association in a typical American evangelical church than I am to find those who advocate for an immigration policy that shows compassion for the immigrant among us? How much of our view on immigration is driven by a political and social agenda rather than a biblical one?

How does anti-immigrant, white privilege bias appear among American Christians? The *Chicago Tribune* reported the story of a dying white congregation (Prospect Heights Community Church) in a Chicago suburb that had received two competing bids from two different churches that were meeting in the church building. One of the bids came from another white congregation (Cornerstone) that had bid $500,000 on the building. The second bid came from a Korean immigrant congregation (Antioch) that had bid $1 million. Despite the huge disparity in the bids, the host church chose to sell the building to the white church for the lesser amount.

At the members' meeting held by the owners of the building that would determine who they would sell the building to, the *Chicago Tribune* reported that the members of Prospect Heights made various disparaging comments about the Korean church. "The remarks included statements that 'Koreans are dirty,' 'Koreans do not clean their site' and 'Korean kids are running around and cannot be controlled,' or words to that effect, in response to which a number of Prospect members cheered."[26] The *Tribune* article goes on to say, "In a subsequent meeting, members of Antioch Korean Covenant Church discussed the vote with the Prospect Heights Community Church council. [In that meeting] the council members didn't deny making the comments but also didn't see anything wrong with them."[27] In a conversation with the pastor of the Korean church, I was told that at the members' meeting where the final decision was to be made, the moderator asked the question "Are we going to sell our building to Cornerstone or to an immigrant church?" To which the congregation united in their vocal support of the sale to the white congregation.

White privilege means that white Christians decide that another white church is more deserving of inheriting a church building, even when their bid is lower than a Korean church's bid. Privilege for the white Christian community is the power to assume what is acceptable and appropriate behavior. Privilege for the white Christian means the assumption that his or her value system, norms, cultural expressions will be the acceptable norm, while "other" cultures will remain on the fringes of American society.

In contrast to the almost desperate clinging to white privilege by Prospect Heights Community Church is Interbay Covenant Church's profound example of laying down power and privilege for the sake of God's kingdom. Interbay was a stable but slowly declining white congregation. They had been hosting a dynamic multiethnic congregation called Quest Church, pastored by Eugene Cho, a Korean American pastor. Ray Bartel, the pastor of Interbay, felt that "the church could go on as it is, but we didn't think that was the right thing to do. Many churches wait until they're nearly dead before they consider coming together. We wanted to do this from a position of strength."[28] So members of Interbay voted overwhelmingly to unite their ministries with Quest.

"As a result, the 54-year-old congregation will give six-year-old Quest a building and land that are mortgage-free and worth an estimated $8 million. The congregations will operate under the Quest name with its leadership team and constitution."[29] Interbay could have continued to maintain their power and privilege over Quest to the bitter end. The pastor and leaders of Interbay could have resisted yielding their name, their status and their building to this much younger church. But instead, Interbay, in an act of obedience and humility, chose to invest, not in a dying Western, white cultural captivity, but in the future of the next evangelicalism.

THE NORM AND EVERYTHING ELSE

In the formation of Christian theology, we also see white privilege at work. Theology that prioritizes the individual and arises out of the Western, white context becomes the standard expression of orthodox theology. In our understanding of what is considered orthodoxy, we see the emphasis on the individual aspects of faith. What is considered good, sound, orthodox theology is a Western theology that emphasizes a personal relationship with Jesus, with its natural and expected antecedent of an individual sanctification and even an individualized ecclesiology. The critical issues and discussion in theology lean toward understanding issues relevant to individuals and Western sensibilities. The seemingly never-ending debate between the proponents of Calvinism and Arminianism, between predestination and free will, revolves around individual salvation.

Theologies that speak of a corporate responsibility or call for a social responsibility are given special names like: liberation theology, black theology, *minjung* theology, feminist theology, etc. In other words, Western theology with its individual focus is considered normative theology, while non-Western theology is theology on the fringes and must be explained as being a theology applicable only in a particular context and to a particular people group. Orthodoxy is determined by the Western value of individualism and an individualized soteriology rather than a broader understanding of the corporate themes that emerge out of Scripture.

Because theology emerging from a Western, white context is considered normative, it places non-Western theology in an inferior position and elevates Western theology as the standard by which all other theological frameworks and points of view are measured. This bias stifles the theological dialogue between the various cultures. "Attendant assumptions of a racial hierarchy that assumes the intellectual and moral superiority of the Caucasians, has hampered our understanding of the text by unnecessarily eliminating possible avenues of study."[30] We end up with a Western, white captivity of theology. Western theology becomes the form that is closest to God. "It is a pretentious illusion that there is something pure and objective about the way theology has been done in the Western church, as if it were handed down directly by the Almighty to the theologians of the correct methodology."[31]

This marginalization of non-Western theology is reflective of Edward Said's description of "orientalism." Said examines Western perceptions of the Orient (in Said's case, he focuses on Arabic and Middle-Eastern cultures when referring to the Orient) and reveals how the exoticizing of "oriental" culture allows Western culture to create a sense of otherness for these cultures. "Orientalism can be discussed and analyzed as the corporate institution for dealing with the Orient—dealing with it by making statements about it, authorizing views of it, describing it, by teaching it, settling it, ruling over it: in short, Orientalism is a Western style for dominating, structuring, and having authority over the Orient."[32]

Creating "the other" allowed Western culture to express its power over non-Western cultures. Inferiority is inferred when a culture or people are categorized as "the other." "European culture gained in strength and identity by setting itself off against the Orient as a sort of surrogate and even an underground self."[33] In the same way that Western culture diminishes non-Western culture through the creation of an "otherness," Western Christianity diminishes non-Western expressions of Christian theology and ecclesiology with the creation of "otherness."

When this sense of "otherness" is created, alienation between the races is created. When "the other" is cast as an exoticized outsider, then it creates a hostile environment for the marginalized person of color. The following story from an Asian American blogger reveals the harmful aspects of the creation of "the other":

> I am sitting in a service at my home church in Missouri. During an announcement for a new outreach to international students, a non-Asian woman dressed in a kimono (traditional Japanese dress) stepped up to the mike. She was an elder's wife. She feigned an accent, in which she spoke in halting English. The congregation roared with laughter. There were two Asians in church that day. One was me. The other was my unchurched friend. He turned to me and said, "This is bullsh__." He got up, turned around (we were sitting in the front row) and walked past the crowd of 800 laughing and guffawing faces.
>
> To my knowledge, he has never stepped into a church again. When he (and I) walked out, it stirred a controversy. Some were concerned that the way we walked out was too militant and not a new testament model of reconciliation. Some were concerned that we were hurt, and needed inner healing. Some were concerned that we didn't get the joke, and did not understand that no harm was intended. Not once was the elder's wife held accountable. The problem, it seemed, was us. Thicker skin, an improved sense of humor, inner healing, less outrage, and a less serious disposition seemed to be the order of the day.[34]

In what ways do we alienate those outside of majority culture? Even as we attempt to engage in crosscultural dialogue and connection, does the system of white privilege and the dominant culture's captivity of the norms of the American church hinder genuine dialogue and true reconciliation?

For instance, what would it look like not to have white theology at the center? There would be more opportunities given to prophetic voices such as Oscar Muriu, Orlando Costas, Emmanuel Katongole, James Cone, Lamin Sanneh, K. P. Yohannan and scores of others. I am thankful for the increasing number of works that examine global theology and the rich history of contribution from non-Western theologians. Can the American evangelical church begin to prioritize works like Samuel Moffett's *Christianity in Asia*, Edwin Yamauchi's *Africa and the Bible*, *The Africa Bible Commentary* edited by Tokunboh Adeyemo, Yeo Khiok-khng's *What Has Jerusalem to Do with Beijing?* and recognize that these works represent not only the next evangelicalism but a historical Christianity as well.

A BIBLICAL UNDERSTANDING OF RACISM

As stated earlier in this chapter, the Bible does not use the category of race the way it is currently employed in American society. However, that does not mean that the Bible is silent on the issue of the sinfulness of racism and the importance of reconciliation. Scripture speaks forcefully about the need for racial reconciliation and racial justice, particularly when racism is viewed in light of our understanding of sin. Racism needs to be seen not only as a social malady that negatively affects American society but also as a biblically defined sin and a result of human depravity and fallenness. Central to our understanding of the sin of racism is our understanding of the image of God and how humanity attempts to usurp God's creation order. Sin results when human beings attempt to take God's place in creation. In other words, we make ourselves the standard of reference in the determination of our values and norms. Racism elevates one race as the standard to which other races should seek to attain and makes one race the ultimate standard of reference.

"It was the distinguishing characteristic of man, that he was created in the image and likeness of God."[35] To be made in the image of God means that humanity "bears and reflects the divine likeness among the inhabitants of the earth, because he is a spirit, an intelligent, voluntary agent."[36] The uniqueness of humanity comes from God's breathing of spirit/life (*ruakh*) into us (Gen 2:7). When Adam received the breath of life, he received for all of humanity the image of God. The breath of life that entered Adam has been passed on so that all of humanity receives from Adam—however warped and distorted—the spiritual image of God. Racism elevates the physical image above the spiritual image of God endowed to us by the Creator. Racism is "idolatry. It is a decisive act of turning away from God to the creature. It is the worship of the creature instead of the Creator (Romans 1:25). Racism is complete deification which . . . elevates a human factor to the level of the ultimate. . . . Large numbers of Christians have failed to identify self-deification in its purest form, namely, racism. Racism alone claims ultimacy for human beings."[37]

The image of God also finds expression in fellowship and community life. Karl Barth finds in the male/female difference: "the original form not only of man's confrontation of God but also of all intercourse between man and man, it is the true humanum and therefore the true creaturely image of God."[38] In Genesis 1:27 we find that humanity is created in the image of God.

God created human beings	in his own image,
in the image of God	he created them;
male and female	he created them.

Genesis 1:27 is written as three lines (tricolon), in the Hebrew poetry style of synonymous parallelism (i.e., the three lines make the same statement in slightly different words). The first line expressed is statement A and statement B, followed by a restatement of A and B in the following two lines. Statement A, "God created human beings," is repeated twice in the following lines as "he created them" and "he created them." Statement B, "in his own image" is repeated as well as "in the image of God" and "male and female." The tricolon parallelism in this verse shows that being created male and female is a part of being made in the image of God. The image of God is reflected not only in the indi-

vidual but also through the creation of both male and female, that is, in community. In this way, human beings reflect God, who exists not as a solitary being but as a being in fellowship.[39]

A sense of fellowship and unity heightens the uniqueness of humans in the creation order. As Barth further asserts, "What distinguishes him from the beasts? According to Gen. I, it is the fact that in the case of man the differentiation of sex is the only differentiation. Man is not said to be created or to exist in groups and species, in races and peoples, etc. The only real differentiation and relationship is that of man to man, and in its original and most concrete form of man to woman and woman to man."[40] The image of God is not limited to a personal application, but also has a corporate application. There is, therefore, an equality and a unity that transcends racial barriers which is inherent in the doctrine of the image of God. To put it into more concrete terms, the image of God means that "we could search the world over, but we could not find a man so low, so degraded, or so far below the social, economic, and moral norms that we have established for ourselves that he had not been created in the image of God."[41]

Racism divides human community by elevating one race as the standard by which all other races should be judged, thereby placing the dominant race in the position of God. It disrupts the image of God in the fellowship of one human to another. Emil Brunner states that since "God . . . creates me in and for community with others . . . the isolated individual is an abstraction . . . the other, the others, are interwoven with my nature. I am not 'I' apart from the 'Thou.'"[42] Racism alienates and separates the "I" from the "Thou" and yields a division of humanity along lines which God did not intend. "Racism is human alienation purely and simply."[43]

If racism's impact is best measured as a sin in light of the image of God, then part of the solution to racism may be found in a proper application of the doctrine of the image of God. If we realize that all of humanity is created in the spiritual image of God and that there is a base equality in humanity's worth derived from God's image as well as equality in humanity's tragedy as fallen beings, then there would be no sense in asserting the superiority of one race over another. And if we as believers are seeking to be more in the image of Christ, then our spiritual striving would not yield differentiation based on race. "To the degree we have progressed in the likeness of our Creator, to that degree we shall be free from class and racial consciousness and discrimination. . . . In this new relation we shall accept one another as members of God's family."[44]

As Christians who seek to proclaim the power of God and his kingdom, we should seek to confront the sin of racism in all its manifestations, for it is an affront to the glory of the God of creation. "Surely the God who created man [sic] in his own image . . . who loved all men enough to give His Son for their salvation, and who taught us to love our neighbor as ourselves, did not and does not intend that any man or any segment of mankind should be kept in permanent subserviency or should be treated as innately inferior, as second-class citizen,"[45] for this is an affront to the God of creation, who made all things and called it good. The white captivity of the church elevates the standards and norms of Western, white culture above all other races and cultures. White captivity usurps God's glorious image in all races by establishing a gradation of value among the races and establishing a system of white privilege and entitlement.

A Multiethnic Evangelicalism

How, then, should the church respond to white privilege and white captivity? Maintaining churches that further propagate white privilege is not the answer. The popular church growth movement in the latter half of the twentieth century (see chapter four for more on this topic) prioritized the homogenous unit principle (HUP) as a method toward numerical growth. Homogeneous churches grow faster because people prefer to attend church with those from similar racial, socio-economic, ethnic and cultural backgrounds. In an attempt to draw individuals into the church, barriers needed to be removed, and that meant that dealing with racial differences which would detract from the real work of church growth would not be considered.

I participated in a roundtable discussion reported in *Christianity To-*

day in 2005, where the influential pastor of Willow Creek, Bill Hybels, confessed that "Willow Creek started in the era when the church-growth people were saying, 'Don't dissipate any of your energies fighting race issues. Focus everything on evangelism.' It was the homogeneous-unit principle of church growth."[46] The homogenous unit principle allowed the white church to further propagate a system of white privilege by creating a system of de facto segregation. Segregation justified by a desire for church growth allows affluent white churches to remain separate.

As the roundtable discussion unfolded, I was thankful for Bill Hybels's willingness to acknowledge the historical misstep taken by Willow Creek in adhering to a set of principles that furthered racial segregation. There were numerous pragmatic reasons to pursue a homogenous unit principle, and acknowledging these priorities was a significant first step in addressing the racial division that resulted from a principle that segregated rather than united. To hear this type of admission from a white leader was both refreshing and encouraging.

Multiethnic churches, and the racial reconciliation and justice needed to establish multiethnic churches, do not mesh with the homogeneous unit principle. Because "racial separation in the United States is socially constructed, the church in the United States reflects a social reality rather than promoting a theological vision."[47] Multiethnic churches that focus on racial justice and reconciliation can result in theologically driven church ministry, rather than economically and pragmatically driven ministry. However, the demographic changes in American society mean that more multiethnic churches are needed in an increasingly ethnically and culturally pluralistic America. "In 1960, less than 15 percent of the population of the United States was not of European origin, with the vast majority of that percentage being African American. According to the 2000 Census, people of color as a percentage of the United States population have *more than doubled* to 31 percent since 1960, and the growth of non-Europeans is expected to continue at an accelerated rate."[48] There is, therefore, an acute need for the planting and development of multiethnic churches in America. "Christian congregations, when possible, should be multiracial. . . . The twenty-first century must be *the century of multiracial congregations.*"[49]

Despite the need for more multiethnic churches, the reality of the situation is that the percentage of multiethnic churches in the United States remains relatively low. American evangelicalism still has not developed enough multiethnic churches. As DeYoung and others reveal:

> If we define a racially mixed congregation as one in which no one racial group is 80 percent or more of the congregation, just 7.5 percent of the over 300,000 religious congregations in the United States are racially mixed. For Christian congregations, which form over 90 percent of congregations in the United States, the percentage that are racially mixed drops to five and a half. Of this small percentage, approximately half of the congregations are mixed only temporarily, during the time they are in transition from one group to another.[50]

Given the rather generous criteria used by the authors, the reality that less than four percent of Christian congregations are integrated is shameful. If we were to hear of any other institution, such as a government agency or an institute of higher education, that was integrated by less than four percent, there would be justifiable outrage and protest. Yet, the American evangelical church marches along in our single-ethnic ministries focused on numerical growth over the biblical value of racial reconciliation and justice.

A major obstacle to the establishment of multiethnic churches is the system of white privilege in the American evangelical church that is a product of white captivity. When the majority culture continues to define and shape the parameters and course of the discussion on what the church will look like, those who are "the other" and who sit outside the halls of power and privilege are silenced, and the multiethnic dialogue deteriorates once again to a white monologue. When the acknowledged leadership, the noted theologians and the model pastors of American evangelicalism are white, then American evangelicalism is captive to white culture. Racial justice, therefore, must be the paradigm by which we build multiethnic churches. Rather than uplifting one race and ethnicity as the ultimate image of God, we must establish churches that honor the breadth of God's image found in a range of cultural expressions.

Throughout American history, there have been numerous images to define American culture as it relates to multiethnicity. In elementary school, I remember seeing a *Schoolhouse Rock!* episode where a catchy tune was coupled with lyrics about "The Great American Melting Pot." The children's show was reflecting a common term that was used when I was in elementary school. The melting pot image claimed that the vast array of rich and diverse cultures that make up America would melt away into an unrecognizable mass of cream of mushroom. All the various flavors would blend into one bland flavor. But I don't remember the melting pot theory being taught too much after elementary school. Somebody had determined that the image doesn't work. Not everyone in America wants to have their unique cultural flavor melted away. As one Native American pastor told me, "There's something in Natives that doesn't melt very well." There was an arrogant presumption that these non-Anglo cultures could be melted away and absorbed into a larger American culture (i.e., white culture).

With the rejection of the "melting pot" image came the advent of the "salad bowl." In the salad bowl, once again, the wide range of flavors was brought together. But the salad allowed for each vegetable to retain its flavor. Unfortunately, we often took this rich array of flavors and drenched it in creamy ranch. The dressing overwhelmed and covered all of the other vibrant flavors. Even a jalapeño or *kimchi* covered in creamy ranch would come out tasting like creamy ranch. We may have all the different flavors in one place, but our style of worship, our style of preaching, and our approach to community life reflect a form of cultural dressing that covers all of the other flavors and drowns them out.

In recent years, the need for the planting and development of multiethnic churches has been recognized among many evangelicals. Among those who are pursuing multiethnic churches, two streams have emerged: the colorblind approach and the racial reconciliation ap proach.[51] The colorblind approach assumes that all believers have their primary identity as Christians; therefore, no concession needs to be made for cultural differences. Since we are all believers, our cultural differences should not matter. In other words, the most effective approach to multiethnicity is to cover everyone in the church with the same flavor of dressing. Usually, the use of Western, white forms of worship, teaching and community are assumed in these types of settings. After all, the "norms" of American church life are assumed; therefore, the common denominator of Western, white forms of ecclesiology becomes the key expression of church life in a colorblind approach.

The racial reconciliation approach asserts that significant sins have been committed related to the issue of race. These sins cannot be avoided or swept under the rug. These historical and social sins need to be dealt with when bringing the range of different races and ethnicities together as a worshiping community. The presence of the social-historical corporate sin of racism cannot be ignored. Between these two expressions of multiethnicity, the colorblind approach fails to acknowledge human fallenness. While the colorblind approach may be efficient and easier, it fails to acknowledge sin and can become a human rather than a divine effort. The racial reconciliation and justice approach moves multiethnicity out of the realm of church growth fad to a level of addressing injustice and sin.

If the American church is going to be prepared for the next phase of its development, then the white captivity of the church that assumes white privilege needs to be cast aside. If the American church is able to look toward the future with a hope and a promise, then the sin of racism must be confessed and racial justice and racial reconciliation become a theological priority over and above the priority of producing a pragmatic paradigm of church growth. To cast aside the Western, white captivity of the church means to look toward a potential of a healthy and dynamic multiethnic future for American evangelicalism.

PART TWO

The Pervasiveness of the Western, White Captivity of the Church

4

The Church Growth Movement
and Megachurches

I LOVE THE ANONYMITY OF VISITING churches on vacation. No one
knows who I am. I can wear the most worn out pair of jeans and even
wear a T-shirt with radical sayings on the front and nobody will say
anything—after all, I'm a visitor. This anonymity also affords me the
privilege to engage the worship service as a participant-observer rather
than a participant-leader (which is my typical role as a pastor). It is easier to learn much about the state of the church in America when it is not
your own church being critically analyzed and it is someone else's
church under the microscope.

Our family was vacationing in a somewhat remote area of the United
States. We obviously didn't know the area well enough to know if there
was a church that fit our preferences, so we picked the church that was
nearest to the motel where we were staying. We got to the church early
(actually on time, but only newcomers seem to arrive at church on time)
and sat in the balcony of a clean, well-cared-for building that had the
capacity to seat about five hundred worshipers. The worship opened
with words of welcome (with most of the emcee's gaze suspiciously in
our direction as we appeared to be the only visitors in the church that
day with about a hundred worshipers in total scattered throughout the

large sanctuary), followed by a blend of worship songs, including a song
I had never heard before: "Roll Out the Spirit," sung to the tune of "Roll
Out the Barrel."

The laid back and informal style appealed to my North American
sensibilities. From the balcony I could see the church members busily at
work helping the service move along in a professional manner. A few
were coming in and out of the sanctuary, maybe checking to make sure
that the bathrooms were sparklingly clean. The soundboard operator
fiddled with the knobs all throughout the service, while conscientious
ushers staffed the doors. The sermon was notable for its lack of direct
scriptural references but was nevertheless rife with humorous illustrations and moving stories. At one point, the pastor took out a real live
hunting bow and arrow to visually demonstrate a biblical point (I can't
remember if the illustration was highlighting trying to hit the right target in your life or that sin was equivalent to missing the mark—on second thought, I seriously doubt it was the latter).

After the sermon, the pastor asked a young couple seated in the front
row to stand before the congregation. The husband was an itinerant
evangelist who had come to lead a series of revival meetings in that
town. The pastor revealed that he was inviting the evangelist and his
wife to stay and lead revival meetings at their church indefinitely. He
then went on to say: "Now this has nothing to do with what that church
down in Florida is doing. We're not trying to copy what they're doing by
inviting a full-time revival preacher. But we do know that that church
grew tremendously. We hope to see the same thing here."

STRANGELY FAMILIAR

When visiting different evangelical churches throughout the United
States, a certain degree of familiarity begins to emerge. While neither a
unifying doctrine nor a common demographic seems to characterize
American evangelicalism, it is still an entity that can be intuited before
it can be quantified. In other words, you can sniff out an evangelical
church even before describing it in great detail. Part of the explanation
lies in American evangelicalism's tendency to copy and imitate success-

ful ministry efforts. If a certain program or paradigm of ministry works in one part of the country, then it must work in another part of the country. If a megachurch in southern California used this particular approach to ministry, then certainly, it can be applied to our small church in Maryland. A church in New York used this methodology to grow their attendance numbers; therefore, the very same methodology can be uncritically applied to our church in Seattle.

Pastors' conferences, books hyping the latest ministry idea, e-mails and other resources serve to provide a uniform range of ideas applied to all churches and ministry contexts. As a pastor, I am painfully aware of the many ways that my ministry falls short (usually in the area of attendance) and compares unfavorably with the many successful churches that I read or hear about. My sermons pale in comparison to what my church members can hear on Christian radio or via iTunes downloads. Our church's programs do not measure up to what another church is initiating. Pressure is applied to churches to mimic or copy the latest fads and programs to become a successful growing church.

Much of this church-in-a-box approach to ministry traces back to the strong and pervasive influence of the church growth movement in the latter half of the twentieth century. Many elements of the church growth movement became standard operating procedure in the local church—affecting and shaping churches, oftentimes without their knowledge or much critical reflection. The effect of this influential movement was felt in numerous local churches throughout North America as they attempted to apply formulas for church ministry across denominations, regions and even across ethnicities. How did this movement, which reached its zenith in the last decade of the twentieth century, attain its high level of influence?

A Short History of a "Big" Movement

The church growth movement of the twentieth century began with the noblest of intentions. The father of the modern church growth movement was Donald McGavran, a missionary to India whose church growth principles arose out of the early twentieth-century missionary zeal for "the evangelization of the world in this generation." From the perspective of both a missionary and an academic, McGavran was attempting to figure out why churches in certain parts of India were growing, while others were not.

In order to expand the missionary efforts and see the fulfillment of the Great Commission, McGavran sought to apply the prevalent social scientific methodology of his time to better understand the disparity in church growth. Employing this modern, social scientific approach, McGavran attempted to answer four major questions:

What are the *causes* of church growth?
What are the *barriers* to church growth?
What are the factors that can make the Christian faith a *movement* among some populations?
What *principles* of church growth are *reproducible*?

McGavran was seeking to scientifically quantify the factors of church growth through a social scientific approach often employed by modern academics and social scientists.[1]

The formation of McGavran's perspective on church growth was largely in response to the fundamentalist-modernist controversy of the early and mid-twentieth century. McGavran studied under H. Richard Niebuhr at Yale Divinity School, who believed that missions was everything that the church did outside its four walls, including philanthropy, education, medical care, evangelism and so forth. McGavran, however, came to believe that evangelism should not be confused with good works and social programs. Reflecting the more fundamentalist view of his time, McGavran believed that all mission activity should be done with a goal toward personal evangelism and individual conversion. By inputting evangelism into the mission of the church, the inevitable outcome would be church growth. McGavran's findings drew the attention of Fuller Seminary, which invited him to become the founding dean of the School of World Mission in September of 1965. His work at Fuller in partnership with C. Peter Wagner gave birth to the classical church growth movement.

The initial propositions of McGavran that form the core principles of the church growth movement are

1. God wants his lost children found and enfolded into the life-giving nature of Jesus. The focus is on the Great Commission and the verbal proclamation of the gospel.

2. The church needs to discover the facts of church growth and research the causes and barriers to church growth.

3. The church needs to develop specific plans based on the discovered facts and set goals and develop strategies to win people to Christ and to plant new churches. Practical plans are needed to make church growth happen.[2]

These core principles tend to emphasize the Great Commission at the expense of the Great Commandment to love the Lord your God and to love your neighbor as yourself. Church growth principles, therefore, prioritized an individualized, personal evangelism and salvation over the understanding of the power of the gospel to transform neighborhoods and communities. They also emphasize a modern, social science approach to ministry, focusing on a pragmatic planning process that leads to measurable success goals. An additional major factor in the misapplication of church growth principles is the decontextualization of principles that worked in an Indian caste society, but did not translate directly to suburban middle-class American culture. As Bill Bishop notes in *The Big Sort*, "Ministers took what was learned nearly a century ago by Christian missionaries trying to overcome the caste system and language barriers in India and applied those lessons to the new American villages appearing on the subdivided plains outside the central cities."[3]

McGavran's classical approach to church growth centered on the academic study of the social sciences in the fields of missiology and ecclesiology in a seminary context, such as the Charles E. Fuller Institute for Evangelism and Church Growth at Fuller Seminary. Increasingly, however, these principles were being applied in a local church context and the themes of the classical church growth movement took on a more popular application. The popularization of the church growth movement meant that practitioners replaced academics as the primary spokespeople and propagators of the church growth movement. Graduates of Fuller Seminary's D.Min. program in church growth, such as John Maxwell and Rick Warren, became the face of the popular church growth movement in the later part of the twentieth century.

As popular expressions of church growth began to dominate American evangelicalism, the megachurch obsession came to the forefront. The models of ministry in the American church became the megachurch pastors, such as Rick Warren, Bill Hybels, T. D. Jakes and Joel Osteen. With the megachurch model becoming the model of evangelical church success, an overwhelming pragmatism began to shape ministry. Literature and resources on church growth became much more practical in nature. These practical approaches and popular church growth paradigms were one step removed from the sociological and theological reflection evident in the early stages of the church growth movement.

Furthermore, the pragmatic paradigms of the popular church growth movement were a generation removed from the context of the fundamentalist-modernist controversy. The cultural context and socio-philosophical discussions of the late twentieth century differed from the contention between church and culture in the early part of the twentieth century. McGavran's push for an overemphasis on personal evangelism was a response to the perceived overemphasis on social justice among the theologically liberal churches. The social gospel came to be seen as an expression of liberal theology in contrast to the individual, personal salvation focus of conservative, fundamentalist churches. This social-historical context to which McGavran was responding did not exist when the popular version of the movement took up the banner of church growth—so that the popular church growth movement was applying paradigms that were more applicable to a previous generation. Furthermore, because of the impact of these megachurches in the late twentieth century, church growth paradigms and popular expression of church growth theory became equated with evangelicalism.

THE CULTURAL CAPTIVITY OF THE CHURCH GROWTH MOVEMENT

The problematic elements of the church growth movement, particularly in its popular expression and application in the late twentieth century, center around how church growth values are held captive to Western, white culture—reflecting the values of individualism, materialism and racism. Popular church growth theory focused on an individualized and personalized approach to salvation. The early roots of the church growth movement began with the emphasis on individual salvation and personal evangelism. This emphasis continues to current times, resulting in an unbiblical divorce of social justice and personal evangelism. "There was a time when evangelicals had a balanced position that gave proper attention to both evangelism and social concern, but a great reversal early in this century [twentieth century] led to a lopsided emphasis upon evangelism and omission of most aspects of social involvement."[4] The church growth movement's imbalanced prioritizing of evangelism over social justice was a reflection of a growing rift in twentieth-century American Christianity, and the individual focus of the church growth movement furthered that rift. The Western value of individualism and personal salvation came to the forefront in the church growth movement, suppressing the value of community and social justice.

The church growth movement's reliance on the modern scientific method is a reflection of the materialism of Western culture. Instead of reflecting on the spiritual factors that led to church growth, the movement focused on pragmatic variables. In addition, the church growth movement propagated a materialistic definition of success, by using consumer statistics (such as attendance figures and budgeted cash flow) as the means of measuring success. As Bob Linthicum states in *City of God, City of Satan*,

> I know of no instrument [church attendance statistics] that creates more guilt and sense of failure in my denomination than this instrument. That is because it favors any church located in a community of rapid growth and radically disfavors any church in a decaying, declining community. The first kind of community is

found mostly in suburban areas of the United States, while the second is found primarily in inner cities.[5]

With American society's prioritizing of objects over people, material success has often been seen as the apex of achievement in American culture. The American church's captivity to market-driven materialism results in greater respect being accorded to bigger and richer churches. The culmination of the captivity of the evangelical church to materialistic values is the church growth movement and the American megachurch.

In addition, the church growth movement's captivity to Western, white culture yields an expression of underlying racism. Under the guise of doing what is best for evangelistic efforts, racial segregation could be justified for the sake of church growth. Couched as a church growth principle, the homogenous unit principle (which emphasizes that churches grow faster when they form along racially homogenous groups) yields a racial segregation that furthers racial conflict and alienation. Blindly adhering to the homogenous unit principle, therefore, has resulted in an American evangelicalism incapable of dealing with the reality of a growing cultural pluralism and ethnic heterogeneity. De facto segregation perpetuated by the church growth movement yielded a disenfranchisement of nonwhites from the larger evangelical movement as Western, white values of success shaped American evangelicalism's perception of success. The church growth movement served the function of furthering the defining of American evangelicalism by Western, white culture.

A Tale of Two Cultures

Another method of analysis of the impact of the church growth movement draws upon the terms proposed by Doug Hall and Judy Hall of the Emmanuel Gospel Center in Boston, Massachusetts.[6] The Halls employ the terms *primary* and *secondary culture*[7] in an attempt to understand cultural dynamics at work in the context of urban missions. The relationship between primary and secondary cultural systems reveals how the misinterpretation of the variable leading to the formulation of church growth theory led to the misapplication of church growth principles.

Nineteenth-century sociologist Ferdinand Tonnies defines primary culture as having the following characteristics:

1. Face-to-face association;

2. The unspecialized character of that association;

3. Relative permanence;

4. The small number of persons involved;

5. The relative intimacy among the participants.[8]

Primary culture is more often found in tribal cultures, where most needs are met through extended family and interpersonal relationships. Sociologist Charles Cooley stresses the centrality of relationships and community in the context of primary systems:

> By primary groups I mean those characterized by intimate face-to-face association and cooperation. . . . The result of intimate association, psychologically, is a certain fusion of individualities in a common whole, so that one's very self, for many purposes at least, is the common life and purpose of the group. . . . The most important spheres of this intimate association and cooperation—though by no means the only ones—are the family, the play-group of children, and the neighborhood or community group of elders.[9]

Oral logic and communication characterize primary cultural systems. Primary systems prioritize relationships, which serve as the basis for learning and social controls. "The ability to operate interrelationally naturally leads primary culture people to be able to generate community itself . . . that is, they are more oriented to people than to things."[10] Because primary cultural systems stress relationships and will oftentimes generate an enclosed system, there is a great deal of security and certainty found in this system. A primary system "bestowed on all its members an unquestioned place and a secure identity. It answered most of the great questions of human existence—marriage, occupation, life goals—almost before they were raised."[11]

In contrast, secondary culture is found in the context of industrial culture, where most needs are met through secondary relationships and systems (structures and institutions). The individual "depends on such a complex net of services to maintain himself in existence in a modern city, the majority of his transactions will have to be public and will be what sociologists call functional or secondary. In most of his relationships he will be dealing with people he cannot afford to be interested in as individuals but must deal with in terms of the services they render to him and he to them."[12] In a secondary culture, an individual can "acquire food, clothing and shelter without really knowing anyone. In a primary culture, that would be impossible, or at least very unusual."[13]

Secondary culture focuses on extrafamilial relationships based on individualism rather than the community, relational focus of primary culture. Written logic and communication characterize secondary cultural systems. Secondary systems, therefore, prioritize production and information, which yield ineffective social controls. Secondary culture is highly individualistic in nature. In a secondary system, "everybody is by himself and isolated, and there exists a condition of tension against all others. Their spheres of activity and power are sharply separated, so that everybody refuses to everyone else contact with and admittance to his sphere."[14]

Primary and secondary cultures yield two very distinct value systems that operate with vastly differing impacts upon society. While most cultures will have expressions of both cultures, one culture will usually be more dominant that the other. The contrast between these two cultural systems can be summarized in the following way:[15]

Primary Culture	Secondary Culture
Tribal culture	Industrial culture
Personal culture—priority of people	Impersonal culture—priority of objects
Survival depends on relationships	Survival depends on knowledge
Extended family	Post-nuclear family
Oral communication	Written communication
Communication is personal and visual	Communication through machines

The following examples may help clarify the distinction between the two cultural paradigms. In primary culture, if someone wants vegetables for dinner, he or she will go to their backyard or a neighborhood garden and bring fresh vegetables to the table—vegetables that had been planted by the person or someone he or she knows personally. In secondary culture, we will go to the nearby grocery store and purchase a bag of precut and prewashed salad and place vegetables in a bowl directly from the plastic bag. We have no idea who picked those vegetables, who cut those vegetables, who washed those vegetables, and we certainly don't know how well those vegetables have been washed. Yet, we serve these vegetables with a high sense of trust that the label is accurate and that none of our loved ones will be ingesting the E. coli bacteria.

In a primary culture, if someone wanted the latest news, he or she would gather around the campfire to hear the tribal elder convey the news. They trusted the news because the elder was someone they knew personally—an uncle, a grandfather or other such relative. In a secondary culture, we watch a complete stranger read the news from a teleprompter, or now more likely, we go on the web to read reports written by individuals who have no real human connection with us. Yet we trust that these reports are accurate because they are written words on a webpage.

Formalized child care in a primary cultural system doesn't exist. Children are allowed to play out in the village because extended family live nearby and they would ensure that the children would be safe. They know and trust all of their neighbors, who are likely to be related to them and, at minimum, will not harm their children. In a secondary cultural system, we cannot trust our neighbor to not harm our kids, much less look out for and care for them. Child care is obtained through agencies found in the Yellow Pages or a nanny webpage. We entrust our most precious gift into the hands of total strangers who have received a seal of approval from other total strangers.

In a primary culture, a conversation with a person would involve walking down the street and sitting at the kitchen table and having a face-to-face conversation—employing nonverbal as well as verbal communication. In a secondary culture, we call our friend on her cell phone at a time we know she will not be available to take the call, so that we can leave a message on her voice mail and in turn she will return the call when we are unable to pick up the phone, so that she can leave us a voice mail. In a secondary culture, two college roommates will be in the same room, their desks on opposite sides of the room, their chair backs almost touching each other and they will be facing away from each other, hunched over their computers, instant messaging each other, instead of simply turning around and talking face to face. Primary culture focuses on human contact and relationships, while secondary culture focuses on productivity and information.

Confusion between primary and secondary culture is part of the inaccurate analysis of the church growth movement. McGavran's use of Western social scientific tools led to the explanation of church growth from a secondary culture point of view, despite the fact that McGavran was examining strongly primary cultural systems. With a secondary culture lens, church growth theory used secondary language and values to describe what is actually primary cultural values at work. A Western bias yielded a system of church growth that missed the real engine of church growth in non-Western cultures: primary cultural systems. The key error in church growth theory is that secondary measurements, such as numerical growth, were used as a central value, rather than attempting to understand the primary cultural dynamics that were at work.

In the popular church growth movement, secondary cultural systems became the means to mass produce and market material to local churches. Programs that could be easily duplicated by the local church captured the imagination of pastors. Discipleship programs that came in a nicely packaged, preset curriculum allowed churches to indulge in the hopes and dreams of the church growth movement without having to delve into the relational messiness that can be primary culture. Oftentimes, when I read popular church growth books, I find the stories of struggle presented by the authors to be the most helpful and real parts of the book. They show how church growth is actually a working through the trials of building a primary culture system. But most of the church growth books deteriorate into the presentation of three principles, a five-step plan or a seven-fold program that will make your church grow. Secondary systems become the way church growth can be duplicated. Secondary systems allow for the mass production and marketing of church growth books that can be haphazardly applied to every local church.

The ultimate expression of secondary culture is the ability to operate with interchangeable parts—with minimal regard for the unique human element in each specific setting. As stated in a recent report in *The Economist*, "Rick Warren . . . likens his 'purpose-driven formula' to an Intel operating chip that can be inserted into the motherboard of any church."[16] Church growth books and theory are oftentimes seen as providing the right software to make the church operate more effectively and efficiently for the sake of church growth. Churches that purchase this program will now be able to duplicate the success of these megachurches and their pastors. Church growth becomes the easy work of installing secondary structures that worked in other parts of the world, rather than the hard work of discovering the primary culture and natural growth that is unique to each local church.

IT'S THE BEST (OR WORST) OF BOTH WORLDS

The twentieth-century popular church growth movement valued and emphasized secondary culture over and above primary culture. The movement reflected a dysfunctional and imbalanced relationship between primary and secondary culture. A healthy intersection of the two cultures yields a healthy system, but an unhealthy intersection yields an unhealthy system. For example, an unhealthy intersection can occur during the transition from primary to secondary culture. A sense of dis-ease can occur, even to the point of creating a dysfunctional system.

Nigerian author Chinua Achebe writes about the destructive experi-

ence of *anomie* (a sense of dis-ease, alienation arising out of social insta-
bility) to a nation transitioning from primary to secondary culture. In
No Longer at Ease,[17] the central character, Obi, is entrusted by his village
to carry on his village's values and traditions (primary culture) while
also representing his community and succeeding in the white man's
world (secondary culture as reflected by the vestiges of the European
colonial system and structures). Obi's navigation through both cultural
systems provides an example of an unhealthy intersection of the primary and secondary culture.

Throughout the book, we see Obi as a noble character attempting to
live out primary cultural values in the face of the overwhelming pressures of secondary culture. Obi is seen as respecting and admiring his
village's culture but also frustrated with their stifling ways. Obi is also
seen as enjoying the pleasures of secondary culture, but angered by its
oppressive nature. When Obi is arrested for taking bribes—even though
that information had been given in the first chapter of the novel—the
reader is still stunned at how quickly this well-intentioned individual
becomes a corrupt criminal.

Achebe reveals how the improper intersection of primary and secondary culture generates the unintended negative consequence of a dysfunctional and destructive system. Other examples of this negative intersection include the Mafia (organized crime), street gangs, and local
political machines. In each of these negative examples, primary systems
(relationships, family connections, blood oaths, etc.) are used as a means
to advance secondary systems (economic gain, bureaucracy, organiza-
tional power, etc.), rather than providing a balance between the two
systems, usually with secondary systems advancing primary culture.
There is a significant danger of misapplying the intersection of primary
and secondary culture to detrimental effect.

However, it is my contention that the *proper* intersection of primary and secondary culture is the key to understanding a healthy,
biblical model of church growth. From a historical perspective, it
can be deduced that primary culture has been the dominant cultural
expression for most of human history, but that there has been a grad-

ual increase of and current dominance of secondary culture, as demonstrated by the following graph (not drawn to scale):

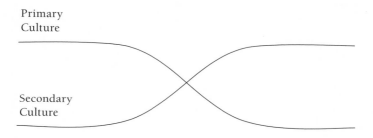

Primary
Culture

Secondary
Culture

Figure 1.

The point of intersection between primary and secondary culture is approximately the time frame of the advent of the New Testament church. The incarnation of Jesus and the establishment of his church occur in the flourishing primary culture of Judaism, but also in the context of a strongly secondary culture of the Roman Empire. The growth of the early church, therefore, gives us an example of the secondary cultural system of the Roman Empire being used to advance a primary cultural system, yielding a healthy system that led to the expansion of Christianity. In *The Rise of Christianity*, Rodney Stark examines the healthy intersection between primary and secondary culture. Subtitled *How the Obscure, Marginal Jesus Movement Became the Dominant Religious Force in the Western World in a Few Centuries*, Stark asks how a thousand Christians in the year A.D. 40 could number close to thirty-four million by the year A.D. 350, comprising over 56 percent of the population. During this time frame, Stark estimates a 40 percent per decade rate of growth.[18]

Stark makes a number of observations that reveal the centrality of primary culture in the early Christian church. Conversions occurred along relational networks; the church's care and concern for their urban neighbors, particularly during times of disease and hardship, led many to convert to Christianity, as well as the presence of a close knit community that cared for one another.[19] At the same time, Christianity arose out of the context of the Roman Empire, which established a strong secondary system (roads, communication structures and a centralized authority) that helped to advance the gospel. News about this compassionate primary cultural system community spread quickly over the existing secondary structures of the Roman Empire. In the early church, exponential growth was a result of a primary cultural system advanced by a secondary cultural system, versus the reverse in a dysfunctional intersection between the two systems.

The early church model of growth discussed by Stark reflects the DNA of church growth revealed in Acts 2. In Acts 2, we see how the church grew at the intersection of primary and secondary culture. This interpretation and application of Acts 2, however, requires rereading the text from a non-Western, nonmodern bias. Most modern, Western interpretation of the Acts 2 passage emphasizes the preaching and public proclamation element of the narrative. Peter's sermon (Acts 2:14-40) serves as the impetus for the growth of the church in Acts 2:41 and 47. Emphasis is placed upon the statement that "with many other words he (Peter) warned them; and he pleaded with them" (Acts 2:40). In most English translations, Acts 2:41 ("Those who accepted his message were baptized, and about three thousand were added to their number that day") is marked off as the culmination of Peter's sermon and not as part of the following section describing the community life of the church. The twentieth century's prioritizing of the sermon as a means of persuasion reflects the importance of preaching and verbal proclamation in evangelism and church growth.

But what if Acts 2:41 serves as a bridge between Peter's sermon and the life of the church as described in Acts 2:42-47? Or what if Acts 2:41 actually belongs structurally to the last section of Acts 2 rather than the first section of Acts 2? If we examine Acts 2:41-47 as one unit, a structure emerges for these verses that points to another explanation for the growth of the church. Acts 2:41 and 47 serve as framing verses for what occurs between Acts 2:42 and 46. The structure of this passage, therefore, follows the *chiastic* structure so commonly found in Greek literature. The passage develops in this manner:

A. Numerical growth of the church (Acts 2:41)
  B. Characteristics of church life (Acts 2:42-43)
    - fellowship (teaching, breaking bread, prayer)
    - outsiders are amazed
      C. Self-sacrificial life of the church (Acts 2:44-45)
  B. Characteristics of church life
    - fellowship (meeting in the temple, breaking bread, praise)
    - outsiders are amazed
A. Numerical growth of the church (Acts 2:47b)

In using the *chiastic* structure, Luke may be pointing to a different interpretation of the growth of the church in the first century. *Chiastic* structures often focus on the relationship between the outside statements' (A) relationship to the center of the structure (C).[20] The center of this *chiastic* structure becomes the focus of how the outside statements come to pass. So instead of seeing evangelism and church growth as the effect of the cause of a verbal proclamation and the preaching of the gospel by Peter, should we instead see evangelism and church growth as a product of the demonstration of the gospel in the self-sacrificial living of the church? Have we overemphasized the personalized, verbal proclamation of the gospel while ignoring the public demonstration of the gospel—through racial reconciliation, social service, social action and justice? Acts 2 points to an evangelism and church growth that incorporates the secondary cultural system of the preached word with the primary cultural system of self-sacrificial living.

The church growth movement of the twentieth century reflects the cultural values of individualism, materialism and racism. The analysis and application of church growth principles reflect a Western bias in biblical interpretation, pragmatism and a leaning toward secondary cultural norms. While examples of church growth are found in Scripture, early church history and global Christianity, our Western bias and the Western, white captivity of American evangelicalism have led to the formation and application of principles that have damaged the church rather than bringing God's shalom to the church.

The Emergent Church's Captivity to Western, White Culture

IT WAS MY UMPTEENTH CONFERENCE on Christianity and postmodernism. For the past few years, I had been hearing so much about postmodernity and the emerging church/emergent phenomena. My favorite Christian magazines and periodicals had given extensive coverage to the key leaders of this movement. I had received brochure after brochure, seen ads in *Christianity Today*, and received countless e-mails advertising the next conference and event about the emerging church. My colleagues in ministry were imploring me to read this book and that book featuring the best young and upcoming pastors, theologians and cultural critics.

So there I was, sitting in yet another workshop led by yet another blonde-haired, perpetually twenty-nine, white male with a goatee. Maybe I should have anticipated the comments of the workshop leader. Maybe I shouldn't have been so sensitive, or needed to develop a thicker skin to these kinds of comments. But the truth is, I'm human and I'm sensitive to insensitivity. The workshop leader was focusing on church planting among postmoderns and the documentation of significant "pomo" churches throughout the United States. As he was listing these exciting "pomo" ministries, I noticed that not a single church on his list was a nonwhite church.

In my quiet, nonconfrontational, Asian American way, I raised my hand.

"Excuse me, but could you talk about some of the pomo church plants in the Asian, Latino and African American communities?"

The workshop leader didn't miss a beat in his answer.

"We have found that there are no Black, Asian or Hispanic pomo churches of any significance."

The American evangelical church tends to be a few steps behind the rest of culture and society. Once evangelicalism grabs a hold of something, however, it tends to add its own unique spin. Contemporary Christian music, online Christian dating services, Christian T-shirts employing commercial logos are some of the examples of the attempt to "Christianize" American culture. In recent years, American Christianity has discovered the term *postmodernity* and has added its own unique evangelical spin. But like much of what has transpired among evangelicals, Christian postmodernity tends to be defined by, geared toward and biased to middle-class, suburban, white America—it reflects the Western, white captivity of the church. Since postmodernity is often seen as simply a response to modernity (a Western construct), it seems natural to see postmodernity as an exclusively Western term and philosophical framework.

American evangelicalism's response to postmodernity has focused on the movement known as the emerging, or emergent, church. With their proliferation, these two terms have lost of lot of their original intent. Generally speaking, they describe a movement of younger, mostly white evangelicals who are challenging the presuppositions and assumptions of a modernity-driven evangelicalism. But as PublishersWeekly .com notes about books with the emerging/emergent church tag, "What it increasingly means is this: The following book was written by a Protestant male under the age of 40. He probably has a goatee. He definitely wears eyeglasses that are much cooler than yours."[1]

Most of the emerging church conversation has focused on postmodernity's impact and role on middle-class, suburban, white churches, resulting in a continuing Western, white captivity of the American church. Evangelical approaches to postmodernity, therefore, are just as captured by culture as ministry to a generation that was raised in the framework of modernity. Because the evangelical perspective on postmodernity is spun from a white, suburban cultural perspective, there is a significant degree of irrelevance to the most significant growth edge in American Christianity—the immigrant of non-European descent, their American-raised children, urban churches and multiethnic churches (i.e., the next evangelicalism).

The movement that has taken on the label of the emerging church has been pronounced the heir apparent to lead the next generation of American Christians. When a national pastors' conference holds a track about the next generation of leaders or the next phase of American evangelicalism, the focus turns to this group of young, white leaders called the emerging church. Emerging church conferences are heralded as the new thing among American churches and emerging church leaders are the leaders to watch. Volumes of books have been written and pages of websites have been created to hype and promote the emerging church. Is this movement deserving of the amount of publicity and promotion it has received?

According to the 2005 book *Emerging Churches* by Fuller Theological Seminary professors Ryan Bolger and Eddie Gibbs, the number of churches and communities that would qualify as emerging in the United Kingdom and United States combined was approximately two hundred.[2] If you were to narrow that list to churches in the United States alone (by generously conceding that more than 75 percent of those churches are in the United States), only about 150 emerging churches would be in the United States. An Internet search (which was part of the methodology used by Bolger and Gibbs to identity these churches) reveals that by 2008, a significant portion of those churches are no longer active. The overall number of emerging churches may be on the increase, but self-identified emerging churches remain a relatively small number. Furthermore, these numbers were significantly smaller when books identifying, and magazine articles highlighting, the emerging church first began to make their appearance.

This relatively small sliver of American Christianity has had undue impact and influence. Given the relatively small number of churches that fit the category of emerging, it is outrageous how many books have been written about the emerging church. Compiling a list of books with an emerging or emergent theme shows over fifty books (and counting) for a group of churches that number one hundred and fifty. In contrast (depending on how you calculate the numbers), there are as many as three hundred to seven hundred churches[3] that are ministering to second-generation Asian Americans. The number of books published by and about Asian American ministry can be counted on one hand. Certainly, there is no comparison in terms of notoriety, publicity and influence.

A list of books published with the Emergent Village imprint in conjunction with Baker Books, Abingdon Press and Jossey-Bass reveals that there are seventeen official publications published by Emergent Village, with every single author being white. A quick glance at the books written for the emerging church reveals the overwhelming number of white male authors in this category. Books by Brian McLaren, Tony Jones and Dan Kimball dominate the list, while nonwhite, nonmale authors are few and far between. Lists of recommended books compiled by emerging church leaders focus on white male authors and leave out nonwhite theologians and contemporary works that focus on ministry in a nonwhite context.

Cornel West, Orlando Costas and Sang Hyun Lee, who have some of the keenest insights on post-Christendom Christianity, are largely ignored. *True Story* by Korean American author James Choung (which reveals an effective method of postmodern evangelism) doesn't merit a mention on the Emergent Village website. Books such as *The Hip-Hop Church* and *Growing Healthy Asian American Churches* are not considered critical reading for the emerging church. Publishers will not market these books to the emerging church and will clump these books with books on immigrant church sociology or release the books in conjunction with Black History Month, while books written by a small group of white males are considered must-reads for any thinking evangelical.

A new thing like Emergent and the evangelical response to postmodernity is as susceptible to the Western, white captivity of the church as
the boomer church and its acquiescence to modernity. The emerging
church casts itself as Western Christianity's response to the Western
philosophical construct of postmodernity. But is it the answer to a
changing culture or a furthering of the Western, white captivity of the
church?

WHAT'S SO POST ABOUT POSTMODERNITY?

"Postmodernism refers to an intellectual mood and an array of cultural
expressions that call into question the ideals, principles, and values that
lay at the heart of the modern mind-set."[4] However, even in its effort to
emerge out of the shortcomings of the Western construct of modernity,
the Christian response to postmodernity remains focused on Western
culture. Postmodernity, as currently being defined in American evangelical circles, becomes an extension of Western culture, oftentimes ignoring the postcolonial, postmonolithic, post-Western, pluralistic world
we now dwell in. The process of deconstructing modernity does not
yield the necessary challenges to the dominant Western paradigm. Instead, it extends the Western modern paradigm and white cultural captivity, but it is now couched in the language of postmodernity rather
than the language of modernity. An African American bloggers explains
why he considers himself to be postemergent by stating: "The conversation still looks too much like the old conversation, white, male and academic. The dominant culture still dominates."[5]

While it is difficult to reduce postmodernity to a set of specific characteristics, there are four attributes of postmodernity that have been
discussed at length by Christian proponents of postmodern ministry:
the demise of an overarching metanarrative, deconstructionism, virtual
reality and pluralism.[6] American evangelicalism has taken these attributes and has applied them in the context of ministry with the corresponding emphasis on community, experience, authenticity and diversity. American evangelicalism is responding to postmodernity with its
own unique application of the postmodern ethos. The postmodern sus-

picion of metanarratives has created an emphasis on community and the micronarratives of local communities; the postmodern expression of deconstructionism has increased the value of experience; the postmodern experience of virtual reality has created a hunger for authenticity; and the postmodern reality of pluralism has yielded a celebration of diversity.

"META-DECON-REALITY" AND THE
EMERGING EVANGELICAL ETHOS

A central aspect of the emerging postmodern generation is the absence of a metanarrative. Modernity was shaped by metanarratives. Enlightenment principles such as the centrality of reason, a linear worldview governed by the Hegelian dialectic, the democratic arsenals' victory over Nazism and Communism, and the triumph of consumer culture are examples of the importance of metanarratives to modernist generations. Postmodernity looks with skepticism at the possibility of an overarching story that governs life. "To the postmodern mind, metanarratives are mere human constructs, fictive devices through which we impose an order on history and make it subject to us."[7] More directly, Jean-François Lyotard writes: "Simplifying to the extreme, I define postmodern as incredulity toward metanarratives."[8]

The demise of cultural metanarratives has yielded a hunger for community on a personal and local level. "Although they have divested themselves of any metanarrative, postmoderns are still left with local narratives."[9] Because local narratives or micronarratives take precedence over metanarratives, postmoderns prioritize local community relationships verses larger metanarrative-driven relationships. "The younger evangelicals yearn to belong to a community."[10] In my years of working with college students, I found that attracting college students to your campus ministry or local church had very little to do with denominational loyalty, how dynamic your sermons were or even the style of worship. College students chose their church based on where their friends were going to church. Community governs postmodern values.

While this hungering for community in response to the loss of metanarratives holds great promise, it must be noted that this emphasis on local communities has furthered white cultural captivity, rather than dismantling it. The stories of the emerging church prioritize the narrative of the white community, thereby creating a new metanarrative out of the local narrative of younger white evangelicals. Furthermore, the deemphasizing of metanarratives has meant the prioritizing of micronarratives (a form of excessive, hyperindividualism), further extending the captivity of the Christian church to the Western value of individualism. Since no unifying metanarrative exists, the influence and impact of the local narrative is determined by the individual, furthering the narcissism and excessive individualism of the Western, white captivity of the church.

A second characteristic of postmodernity is found in deconstructionism, which can be seen as a byproduct of the loss of the metanarrative. "Postmodern thinkers no longer find this grand realist ideal tenable. . . . They contend that we have no fixed vantage point beyond our own structuring of the world from which to gain a purely objective view of whatever reality may be out there."[11] One's own personal interpretation based upon experience and environment is the only true interpretation of text. "The postmodern condition thus pertains to one's awareness of the deconstructibility of all systems of meaning and truth . . . [and] is therefore one of undecidable and unfinalizable interpretation."[12]

Deconstructionism means that the modernist tendency to view the individual simply as a rational being no longer applies. "Postmoderns look beyond reason to nonrational ways of knowing, conferring heightened status on the emotions and intuition."[13] Since our understanding of the world and of the text is not reduced simply to reason and logic, other areas of human life, particularly experience, become important in understanding our world.

Postmodern evangelicals, therefore, explore alternative means of communication, recognizing that truth is not simply communicated through the spoken or written word. "They more readily embrace the more emotive, imaginative, and symbolic forms of communication (without rejecting the significance of the spoken word)."[14] Postmodern generations have a wide range of entertainment options. The communication of truth is not limited to a thirty-minute monologue, but also happens through three-minute YouTube snippets, blogs, instant messaging, Facebook, etc. A friend of mine who toiled away as a field reporter for many years got his break not by breaking a big story on the local news but through a YouTube video that got significant play.

The recognition of the importance of experience and the appropriation of nonverbal communication can have positive implications for ministry to postmodern generations. However, the prioritizing of experience may ultimately result in negative consequences. In the prioritizing of experience, it is significant *whose* experience becomes prioritized. If the experience of the middle-class, white Christian becomes the experience by which other experiences are measured or becomes the experience that is placed front and center of the movement, then we have once again capitulated to the white captivity of the American church.

The third characteristic of postmodernity provides more of a description rather than a prescribed characteristic. Postmoderns must deal with the reality of living in a seemingly virtual world. "Instead of the scientific discovery of the Enlightenment, we now have virtual reality. . . . Since our senses perceive the world differently, each individual's view of reality will be unique. . . . Our world today finds it harder and harder to distinguish fact from fiction."[15] The line between what is reality and what is make-believe has become blurred. Popular culture is rife with examples. Rapid images displayed on the screen replace actual human contact. "Reality" television portrays "real" people in the most unreal of circumstances. Postmoderns, therefore, "live in a world in which the distinction between truth and fiction has evaporated. Consequently, they become collectors of experiences, repositories of the transitory, fleeting images produced and fostered by the diversity of media forms endemic in postmodern society."[16]

Virtual reality affects how an individual views his or her world and in turn affects what that individual will desire. "Instead of heightening our experience of reality, the simulated world of image-enhanced hyperreality distances us from reality and is ultimately unsatisfying and desensitizing. There is something routinely numbing about all of this. Simulation never provides long-term stimulation."[17] What postmodern generations long for, therefore, is in contrast to the virtual reality created by machines and computers. "The shift among younger evangelicals is toward being real and authentic. . . . They just want people to be real."[18] Authenticity becomes a high value to the postmodern generation. The question shifts from Is it true? to Is it real?

The quest for authenticity is a valid attempt to address the postmodern struggle with virtual reality. However, similar to the previous two examples of the evangelical response to postmodernity, the evangelical response to virtual reality through the quest of authenticity can also deteriorate to the furthering of Western, white captivity. The desire to be authentic without the concomitant expression of diversity can lead to authenticity expressed exclusively through a white, Western perspective. If the white voice dominates the dialogue, then the only "real" voices and "authentic" point of view that is acknowledged resides with the white community. The authenticity desired by a nation caught up in virtual reality becomes nothing more than a furthering of a white evangelical agenda seeking to authenticate the middle-class, suburban, white American experience and culture.

PLURALISM AND THE CELEBRATION OF DIVERSITY

The three characteristics outlined above point to how a discussion of postmodern philosophy and the evangelical response to postmodernity yields the furthering of white captivity, especially when the voices heard are limited to those arising from an existing white cultural captivity and from the dominant white culture. Ironically, one of the central tenets of postmodernity is the acknowledgment of the reality of pluralism and the celebration of diversity. Unfortunately, the emerging church has inadequately addressed this central characteristic.

Postmodernity emerges in a world that is increasingly connected on a global level. American culture is now shaped by the plurality of worldviews arising out of globalism. "The postmodern consciousness, therefore, entails a radical kind of relativism and pluralism . . . [and] the central hallmark of postmodern cultural expression is pluralism."[19] Postmoderns recognize that the world has changed since the onset of Eurocentric, Enlightenment-driven modernity. Postmoderns understand the give-and-take of cultures that adds to the heterogeneous reality of the current political, social and cultural systems. As Grenz summarizes, "Postmoderns contend that . . . we must come to grips with the realization that we inhabit a globe consisting of 'multiple realities.' Different groups of people construct different 'stories' about the world they encounter."[20]

Interestingly, while pluralism is almost universally acknowledged as a central tenet of postmodernity, there appears to be minimal appreciation or application of pluralism in the postmodern expression of evangelical Christianity. While copious volumes are being devoted to how community, experience and authenticity are shaping the emerging church, there seems to be a limited understanding of the role of diversity. As Christianity becomes less white and less Western in the twenty-first century, nonwhite and non-Western perspectives must increase in influence. However, reading through works on Christian approaches to postmodernity reveals that diversity is referred to, but very rarely applied.

Brian McLaren's seminal work *A New Kind of Christian* has a chapter titled "Yeah, but What About the Other Guys?" which explores the topic of other religions.[21] The focus of pluralism seems to be about competing worldviews offered by other religions, but no part of the book addresses how nonwhite Christians will influence American evangelicalism. Jimmy Long states that "due to increasing globalization, this emerging culture will have even more of an impact throughout the world."[22] While it is true that Western Christianity in its postmodern expression will continue to influence global Christianity, there seems to be minimal acknowledgment about how Western evangelicalism will be impacted by what is occurring in Christianity throughout the world. Pluralism is being examined from the perspective of how other faiths impact Christianity and how the emerging postmodern evangelicalism will shape the world, but less is said about how nonwhite Christianity will shape American evangelicalism. There is minimal or no recognition of the reality of the next evangelicalism. As in the case of the workshop leader discussed at the beginning of this chapter, nonwhite Christians are not perceived as significant contributors to the evangelical postmodern dialogue.

While diversity is appreciated and sought in secular postmodernism, American evangelicalism has failed to appreciate the critical and central role of diversity to the emerging postmodern generation. A 2004 *Christianity Today* article points out that the emerging church is "overwhelmingly white."[23] As was the case for modern Christianity for the last four hundred years, the recognized voices continue to be white, Western voices. The 2005 National Pastors Convention featured one nonwhite speaker out of the twenty-eight featured speakers for the Emergent Church segment. The 2008 Great Emergence National Event sponsored by Emergent Village featured one nonwhite speaker out of the thirteen featured presenters. African American pastor Karen Ward was the lone nonwhite speaker at both events. [24] Even a cursory examination of the books written in the genre of the emerging church in America reveals that every single author of the fifty-plus books is white. The failure of the American evangelical approach to postmodernity is that it does not address the critical role of diversity and continues to put forth only white faces and voices as representative of the emerging church movement.

The trajectory of the emerging church, therefore, is biased toward those who are the most recognizable voices in the conversation. Even in a conversation, the possibility of one voice or one point of view drowning out another is very real. Racial justice, which runs deep and wide for many people of color, can be relegated to a side issue by whites who are committed to other, more "critical" issues related to postmodernity. As one emergent blogger notes:

> Any study done of churches that claim to be emergent are going to show that they're over 90% white. My own experience of trying to start a conversation with over 80 cohort leaders and over 300 local folks by sending out an email, asking them to read and comment on my first post regarding race and the emergent movement got no

response. Not one comment. I put less effort soliciting comments on the quilt I made and got 8 responses.[25]

Dialoguing on race for most white emergents becomes a luxury, not a necessity, as it is for many people of color.

The great promise of postmodernity is that previously silent voices will be given the opportunity to speak. Modernity silenced minority voices in order to uphold the grand Enlightenment, Eurocentric narrative. Postmodernity, however, seeks to hear voices outside of the dominant white American culture. "A characteristic feature of postmodern debates in a variety of cultural arenas is the insistence on the hearing of alternative voices. . . . In this critique of dominant cultural institutions . . . we are now hearing from those previously voiceless, invisible and unrepresented."[26]

One of the current failings of the emerging church is the failure to listen to other voices. If American evangelicalism is to impact postmodern culture, genuine consideration must be given to nonwhite perspectives and voices that may not follow the main stream of emergent thinking. As Anthony Smith, one of the African American leaders within the emergent conversation who blogs at <postmodernegro.wordpress.com> states, "There is some sense that emergent is hermetically sealed, something completely and wholly new. There needs to be recognition that the emerging church is still a child of larger North American Christianity. This lack of awareness leads to some unconscious racial habits. Because of the social location of most of those involved in emergent, there is an inability to see that."[27]

In the same way that postmodern philosophers decry the tendency of modernity "to smooth out heterogeneous elements in order to secure the appearance of homogeneity in history,"[28] the emerging church has shut out nonwhite voices in their ability to engage on the issue of race. As postmodern philosopher Michel Foucault asserts, this type of usage of knowledge and power constitutes an act of violence.[29] The physical violence of colonialism has been replaced by the social and psychological violence of Western, white cultural captivity.

WHOSE TABLE IS IT?

The emerging church remains predominantly white, but to their credit, the rhetoric of diversity can sometimes be heard. Oftentimes, the defense of the emerging church is to claim that there are a number of nonwhite voices as part of the larger movement. But to what goal is there an attempt to include nonwhite voices? As an individual that is often asked to participate in conferences and institutions that are dominantly white, I struggle with the experience of feeling like the token minority. I have found that there is usually a test to discern the difference between an institution that dabbles in tokenism versus an institution that is committed to genuine diversity. Tokenism means that people of color are invited to strengthen existing systems and further the captivity to the dominant culture.

For example, there is a difference between a seminary or a Christian college that hires one or two minority faculty because it will strengthen their ability to continue to minister to their white constituency and a seminary or Christian college that hires minority faculty to lead the transformation of their institution to become a completely new entity— one that values and exemplifies genuine diversity. Tokenism furthers the existing power structures and the systems of privilege (but now with a few colorful additions), while true diversity looks toward a future beyond Western, white cultural captivity. My hope for the emerging church is that, rather than using nonwhites to pepper the existing framework of Western, white postmodern thought, that diversity will become a central value and manner by which the emerging church relates to American society.

In my first year at Gordon-Conwell Theological Seminary, there was a significant influx of Korean American students. The student population of the seminary, which had been home to a handful of Korean Americans, saw an increase of the Korean student population to about 15 percent of the student body. This spike was most noticeable in the cafeteria, where large groups of Korean and Korean American students would sit together at one or two tables while white students would sit at other tables. This segregation was noticed by several of the white students at the seminary who found this situation to be disquieting. They approached several of the Korean students with the intention of remedying this racial division. Their solution was to ask the Korean students to make an effort to sit at tables comprised of all white students. When the Korean students asked why there wasn't an effort by the white students to come sit at a table comprised of Korean students, the white students responded by saying, "Well, we wouldn't feel comfortable doing that." No concern was given, however, to the fact that Korean students may feel just as uncomfortable sitting at a table comprised of white students.

Too often, ethnic minorities are asked to put aside their discomfort to come and sit at the white table. The rules of the table have already been set and there's not a whole lot of room, but come and sit at *our* table. We won't change the way we interact with one another and we will need to maintain the white majority, but it still would be nice to have an Asian face or a black face sit at *our* table. If the places at the table are already set, and ethnic minorities are asked to put aside their comfort to join an already existing power dynamic and structure, then we are not engaging in genuine ethnic diversity. Ethnic minorities are being asked to play the role of the token minority who should be seen but not heard, rather than those who have wisdom and experience to transfer to the emergent community.

THE TRIUMPH OF MODERNITY

In the transition from modernity to postmodernity, the emerging church continues to call for the forsaking of the trappings of modernity. To forsake modernity, however, means to forsake many of the defining characteristics of American evangelicalism. "Evangelicalism shares close ties with modernity. A child of the Reformation, pietism, and revivalism, the evangelical movement was born in the early modern period. And North American Evangelicalism reached maturity in the mid-twentieth century—at the height of the modern era."[30] How will the American evangelical church cope with this transition after investing so heavily in the modernist mindset? Middleton and Walsh liken the fall of modernity to toppling of the tower of Babel:

But modernity, like Babel, has faltered and is about to topple. The homogeneity of the modern worldview has fragmented into tribalism, gender wars, racial tension, ethnic cleansing and widespread cultural confusion. The sacred canopy of the progress myth that gave us a normative historical orientation is ripped to shreds, and we are left with the tatters of disorientation and anomie. The shared language of the Enlightenment rationality, technical efficiency and economic growth has been drowned out by the deafening cacophony of the postmodern carnival. And like the builders of Babel, we experience the human family as profoundly scattered in its diversity and are fundamentally unable to hear with compassion the voice of the other.[31]

As Babylon (the eventual successor to the tower of Babel) begins to fall, how will evangelicals respond? Will we respond as in Revelation 18? When we who have "committed adultery with her and shared her luxury see the smoke of her burning, [will we] weep and mourn over her" (Rev 18:9)? Or will we see the hand of God moving in our culture to bring his kingdom—a kingdom with no end and a kingdom that draws together all races and ethnicities.

What is the "Babylon" that needs to fall? Is it simply America's captivity to modernity? Or is it an imbalanced dynamic of power that gives greater authority and respect to ideas and principles that emerge out of a Western, white framework? Will tearing down the tower of Babel that is modernity release American evangelicalism from Western captivity, or is the emerging church a furthering of Western, white captivity? If the emerging church continues a Western, white cultural captivity, then the much-needed fall of the tower of Babel and the collapse of Babylon is merely the collapse of modernity. However, what is needed is not merely the collapse of modernity, but the collapse of the Western, white captivity of the American evangelical church.

BIBLICAL REFLECTION ON THE FUTURE OF THE "EMERGING" CHURCH
Hope for the restoration of the unity that was lost at the tower of Babel

and the destruction associated with the impending downfall of Babylon may be found in the biblical example of Micah 4. The passage reveals the future glory of God's people that will be revealed in the last days. With the reestablishment of the mountain of the Lord's temple and the end of conflict and war, many nations will stream to the mountain of the Lord to receive teaching (Mic 4:1-3). Micah 4 promises the reverse of the curse of the tower of Babel. The image of a multitude coming from a diversity and plurality of people groups reveals the polar opposite image of the tower of Babel. Instead of a scattering of people along cultural, ethnic and language differences from the ultimate expression of human hubris, there is a new unity of all peoples gathered at the mountain of YHWH. The gathering at the mountain of the Lord reflects God's longing to restore and gather a shalom community under his power and presence. God desires to restore the unity of humanity that had been lost at the tower of Babel. His longing is for his people to reflect a unity in the midst of diversity.

Yet, the reality of the American church in the twenty-first century is that we are nowhere close to being the united community of Micah 4. Instead, segregation and division continues in the church and we continue to remain captive to Western, white culture. The promise of Micah 4 has not yet found fulfillment. Is the Micah 4 community a possibility? What actions led to the establishment of this community? The key action of the people of God that leads to shalom appears to be the willingness to lay down their swords and spears. The laying down of the sword is a willingness to lay down power for the sake of the shalom community. Reversing the curse of the tower of Babel requires the laying down of power by the people of God. The beginning of this reversal finds its biblical fulfillment in Acts 2 at Pentecost and the coming of the Holy Spirit. People from all different cultures and languages are in Jerusalem and hear the gospel in their own language and the reversal of the curse of the tower of Babel culminates in the gift of tongues, once again uniting God's people under one language.

The challenge of postmodern ministry would be to live out the unity in the midst of diversity found at Pentecost, rather than mourning the collapse of Babylon. Babylon needs to fall. The Babylon that must fall is not merely modernity (as the "emerging" church might contend), but rather, the Babylon that must fall is white cultural captivity. The fall of Babylon, therefore, requires the tearing down of the white dominance of American evangelicalism. The Micah 4 image of a restored unity requires the laying down of power by the people of God. Is the white-dominant emergent community willing to lay down their power for the sake of the unity that needs to emerge out of the diversity in the next evangelicalism?

A few years ago, I was asked to participate in a panel discussion on the church's response to postmodernity. I very rarely get invited to speak at emergent gatherings (actually, I was not invited by the emerging church participants and organizers but instead was asked to participate by a white colleague who had originally been asked). The panel would feature some of the most recognizable names in the emerging church and I would be the only nonwhite participant with three other emergent thinkers. The conversation turned to the problem of globalization. The conversation became heated as the white participants vigorously engaged in a dialogue on the need for the emerging church to deal with the problem of globalization. I stayed silent during the twenty- to thirty-minute argument about how to fix the problem of globalization. The moderator noticed that I had been silent and asked for my take on the situation. My response was direct but not very tactful: "White people talking to other white people about a problem white people created in the first place—why would I care about that conversation?"

I personally find the use of the term "emerging church" to be offensive. I believe that the real emerging church is the church in Africa, Asia and Latin America that continues to grow by leaps and bounds. I believe that the real emerging church is the hip-hop church, the English-speaking Latino congregation, the second-generation Asian American church, the Haitian immigrant church, the Spanish-speaking store-front churches and so forth. For a small group of white Americans to usurp the term "emerging" reflects a significant arrogance. Is there recognition of the reality of the changing demographics of American Christianity? Is there willingness to move beyond the Western, white captivity of the church to a more multiethnic leadership?

If you examine the background of many of the emerging church pastors and leadership, you will find that a significant number are emerging out of a disgruntlement with baby boomer evangelicalism.[32] When emerging white evangelicals were leaving these boomer generation churches, one option that may not have been seriously considered was the opportunity to join African American or immigrant churches. Instead, emerging white evangelicals chose to cluster with other white Americans to form a new movement. Was there a willingness to yield the power and privilege of the Western, white captivity of the American church and explore leadership outside of the white community? Is there now a willingness to yield to leadership outside of the Western, white captivity of the church?

Despite my criticism of the emerging church, I find signs of hope. One of the key (if not *the* key) leaders of the movement, Brian McLaren, is striving to better understand and learn from global Christianity. As he reflects in a recent *Leadership Journal* article:

> The U.S. can so easily become an echo chamber, Western voices arguing with other voices about Western topics from a Western perspective. So I've been devouring books by authors like Rene Padilla, Alan Boesak, Emmanuel Katongole, Jon Sobrino, Mabiala Kenzo and Leonardo Boff. . . . As I read brothers and sisters from the global South . . . my sense of what *missional* means is irrevocably deepened, broadened, transformed.[33]

In a phone conversation with Anthony Smith, my hopefulness is extended when he reminds me that the emerging church has better tools to deal with the issue with diversity. There is a greater openness to engage in conversation on these issues.

I believe that there are aspects of postmodernity that offer great promise to take the issue of racial justice and the white captivity dialogue to a deeper level. I am encouraged by admonishments by those within the movement as reflected in this blog entry by an emergent cohort leader:

We cannot simply wait for non-white folks to come to us. They would only be tokens if we did. We must go out and get them, welcome them, and let them change the agenda so that it more accurately reflects the concerns of the entire Post-modern Kingdom of God, not just the white post-Evangelical, post-Christendom, post-colonial folks. Alternately, we should consider going to them, submitting to their leadership and learning about emergence from folks that have arguable been in the midst of it longer than the white folks have.[34]

Can the crown prince of American evangelicalism decide that instead of trying to solve all of the world's problems from a position of power and privilege, it will listen and learn from the poor in our global village, the marginalized voices, even the angry voices and join in the ministry of the real emerging church—the next evangelicalism?

The Cultural Imperialism of the Western, White Captivity of the Church

ABOUT A HALF MILE FROM OUR SEMINARY CAMPUS on the north side of Chicago, at the corner of Pulaski Avenue and Lawrence Street, is an urban shopping center anchored by Staples and Starbucks—two icons of corporate America. But the busiest store in this complex is actually the store that has a twelve-foot-tall inflatable chicken straddling its roof. It is a chain restaurant called Pollo Campero, a business whose story presents an interesting case study of globalization and Western cultural hegemony.

Many years ago, Kentucky Fried Chicken (now known as KFC) began to establish franchises in numerous locations outside of the United States. In Guatemala, a local businessman responded to this global fast-food craze by opening a fast-food chicken restaurant called Pollo Campero. If you were to close your eyes and taste Pollo Campero chicken, you would recognize the taste as a pretty good imitation of KFC chicken. In recent years, this chain of Pollo Campero restaurants has arrived in the United States as the illegitimate grandchild of KFC. Or put another way, "it is now impossible to isolate the process of the real, or to prove the real."[1] Postmodern philosopher Jean Baudrillard speaks of the elevating of copies above the original. At what point do we begin to confuse the copy with the original? In an increasingly global world, the copy becomes harder to distinguish, but this does not diminish the power of the original to shape culture.

Pollo Campero, Pinkberry (a South Korean export version of frozen yogurt restaurants in the vein of TCBY) and Beard Papa's (Japan's answer to Dunkin' Donuts) are names you may already be familiar with (definitely if you live in California, but even if you live in the Midwest). As Joel Stein of *Time* magazine says: "After its first lap, globalization gets really interesting. The stuff you invented—in this culinary case, fastfood hamburgers, fried chicken, pizza and doughnuts—gets sent out into the world, is replicated by other countries and then comes back to you all crazied up, like a giant game of telephone."[2] With globalization, the western hemisphere's hegemonic stranglehold on culture has taken on a whole new dimension.

GLOBALIZATION AND CULTURAL HEGEMONY

Globalization means that one nation's cultural values and paradigms now have the capacity to infiltrate and affect the entire global community. In terms of potential, globalization offers a great promise and hope. As Thomas L. Friedman explains in *The Lexus and the Olive Tree*, "Globalization involves the inexorable integration of markets, nation states, and technologies to a degree never witnessed before—in a way that is enabling individuals, corporations and nation-states to reach around the world farther, faster, deeper and cheaper than ever before."[3] Globalization means that cultural exchange and influence can occur more frequently and on a much larger scale.

The great promise of globalization is that individuals, people groups and nations can now share their culture, their values and their way of life with others in a proactive and positive way. Advances in technology, transportation and communication create a system of globalization that gives us the potential to enter into a truly multicultural world, where every culture has a worth and a value that is being shared in a newly emerging global culture. The Japanese value of harmony and unity is preached as much as the Western value of the rugged individual. The

Confucian value of respecting elders has equal standing with the American tendency toward worshiping youth culture. By finding the redemptive value of non-Western cultures, we move toward a healthy globalization trajectory.

However, the reality of globalization is that one culture, one nation or one worldview tends to dominate the world, and there is an imbalanced flow between cultures. "Culturally speaking, globalization is largely, though not entirely, the spread of Americanization—from Big Macs to iMacs to Mickey Mouse—on a global scale."[4] Instead of an idealized globalization, we see a cultural hegemony—the imposition of the culture of the powerful upon the powerless. Cultural hegemony is the power and ability by the West to impose its cultural views upon the rest of the world. It describes the way Coca-Cola, Starbucks and McDonald's make their presence felt in all corners of the globe.

Questions are raised whether this transmission of Western culture ultimately usurps indigenous culture and forces an assimilation of non-Western nations into paradigms and systems established by Western culture. In other words, in culture, business and politics, globalization has yielded the Western, white captivity of global culture. "The challenge in this era of globalization—for countries and individuals—is to find a healthy balance between preserving a sense of identity, home and community and doing what it takes to survive within the globalization system."[5]

In the same way, questions may be raised about how the Western, white captivity of the church is transmitted to non-Western expressions of Christianity, resulting in a global Christianity that is just as captive to Western, white Christianity. In the history of world missions, one of the most significant concerns is the paternalism and cultural insensitivity that may be a part of the missionary enterprise. Because of an existing imbalance of power, the movement of the gospel message from Western culture to non-Western culture yields a system of dependence and results in a cultural hegemony.

The difficulty is when not only the gospel message is being transmitted from the powerful to the powerless, but when all the additional cultural baggage is also transmitted from the powerful to the powerless. Because of the imbalance of power, the receptor culture is oftentimes unable to discern or distinguish between the gospel message and the Western, white cultural captivity of the church. While adaptation may occur, this adaptation may focus on furthering Western, white cultural captivity, rather than contextualizing and translating the message of the gospel. As a consequence, the ecclesiology that is mimicked in non-Western cultures may look like a carbon copy of Western models of ministry. Many non-Western seminaries and Bible colleges, for example, approach the training of pastors using the modern paradigms of education that no longer apply, even in the West. In Thailand there are four Bible colleges that require training in Western music, with some schools requiring piano and guitar.[6] The simplistic adapting of Western seminary curriculum to non-Western contexts reveals the holding to Western cultural norms even if they are not relevant or applicable in non-Western culture.

It is important to note once more that this Western cultural hegemony of the church is in contrast to the demographic reality of global Christianity. As Jenkins reminds us, in this increasingly globalizing world, there will be some surprising developments. "Soon the phrase 'a White Christian' may sound like a curious oxymoron, as mildly surprising as 'a Swedish Buddhist.' Such people can exist, but a slight eccentricity is implied."[7] Yet the cultural norms of global Christianity still reflect a Western, white cultural bias and there is a great "need to reduce the imperialistic influence of . . . Western culture in non-Western local churches and lands."[8] Western Christianity continues to export a culturally captive form of Christianity that often becomes the norm of non-Western expressions of Christianity.

WHAT WE EXPORT

When I was a pastor in Cambridge, our church made several short-term mission trips to Romania. I had grown to love and respect a nation that had emerged out of the tremendous conflict and persecution of a ruthless Communist dictatorship. The people of this nation had persevered and were now open to the gospel for the first time in a long time. Our church was hoping to develop a long-term relationship with a church in Severin, Romania. Severin is a small town on the western part of the country, near the Danube River and across the border from the former Yugoslavia. Unlike the larger cities in Romania, such as Bucharest and Timiswara, larger Western mission agencies do not pay much attention to Severin. Severin is literally a dying community. It is home to one of only two hard water treatment facilities in all of Europe, the other being Chernobyl. As a result of the presence of nuclear radiation, everything is dying in Severin. There is tremendous poverty in this town. The town had once had a flourishing economy based on agriculture (mainly very vibrant apple groves), but because of the presence of nuclear waste in the soil, you can drive around the town and see barren fields with trees withering before your eyes. There is a very high rate of infertility. One estimate given to me by a local resident was that about a third of the women in the area were infertile. This estimate was confirmed by a sampling of the rate of infertility of the women in the church. Furthermore, there was a history of deep racial conflict in Severin. Romania has the highest number of gypsies (*Romas*) in Europe (a disputed number ranging from five hundred thousand to two and a half million).[9] The *Romas* are an alienated and persecuted population. Deep-seated animosity and racism is directed toward the gypsy *Romas* by the Romanians.

How should the gospel relate to this unique cultural context? There is no easy answer, but here is the reality. The global cultural flow has already occurred even in this remote Romanian town. The larger churches in Timiswara, shaped by megachurches in the United States, have shaped these small churches in Severin, so that their main approach to ministry reflects prosperity theology. The teaching of the pastors mimicked the big churches in Timiswara, which mimicked the teaching content of a megawatt smiling pastor of an American megachurch. When I visited the churches in Severin, I would often be subjected to health-and-wealth preaching—while all around me, there was overwhelming evidence of the need for a kingdom gospel of justice and reconciliation. So the question is raised: in an era of the Western captivity of the church, is it possible for there to be mutual, reciprocal global cultural traffic? Or are we consigned to an asymmetrical global cultural exchange due to the hegemony of Western Christianity and consequently, Western culture?

TRANSMITTING SINFUL PATTERNS

It was one of the most disturbing news items of 2007. A group of Korean missionaries had been captured by the Taliban and held for ransom. I remember being shocked and horrified that my brothers and sisters in Christ would be subjected to such treatment. I discussed with friends and wrote blog entries on the seeming absence of concern by the Western media (even the American Christian media) and the minimal coverage given the Korean hostages. When the hostages were released, there was great joy, but there was also tremendous sorrow over the loss of lives, as two of the missionaries were killed by the Taliban.

Once the dust settled, I began to reflect upon what events and circumstances led to the kidnapping and murder of these Korean missionaries? Some concerns were raised that the method and approach of the missionary efforts coming out of the churches in Korea arose from a spirit of competition among the churches. Korean churches were trying to outdo each other in radical, risky missionary efforts, in order to market their church more effectively. The materialistic, consumeristic approach to church had influenced the Korean church's approach to church growth and missions. Whose pattern did the Korean churches follow? What examples were presented to these Korean churches that would lead them to see the building up of their church as a competitive market venture?

I do not mean to imply that Koreans are incapable of being materialistic or capitalistic of their own accord. Nor am I stating that without the influence of the American church the Korean church would have behaved differently. But I am asking: "How has Western, white cultural captivity shaped global Christianity?" All human cultures have a propensity to sin, but how is the propagation and the imbalanced cultural flow leading to a global church following dysfunctional patterns of the American church?

The proliferation of prosperity theology in Africa finds its roots in the American prosperity movement. As *Christianity Today* notes, "The worst brand of African prosperity teaching is, perhaps unsurprisingly, an American export."[10] The bishop of one of the more influential prosperity-oriented churches is a graduate of the Morris Cerullo School of Ministry in San Diego, California.[11] Again, I am not implying that there is a pure culture in Africa that is tainted only by virtue of its contact with Western culture. But the seemingly unlimited capacity and potential of the Western church to propagate their ideas at a much faster rate, and the responsibility that comes with this level of power, needs to be examined.

The Western, white captivity of the church involves the multiplication of Western models of ministry for export on a global scale. The secondary systems, that make duplication possible, become the means by which Western, white norms of Christianity become normative for all Christians everywhere. The Western, white captivity of the church is not just an American evangelical phenomenon; it has now become a global phenomenon. The great irony is that churches in the developing nations and among many ethnic minority communities in the United States are among those that are now the best examples of cultural captivity. Can the nonwhite churches recover a sense of God's unique expression through their own cultural context?

BIBLICAL RESPONSE

Humanity was made in the image of God. While our Western individualism will focus our attention on the personal reflection of the *imago Dei* in the individual, we need to see the image of God expressed as a corporate reflection (see chapter three). An understanding of the image of God through a corporate, community context reinforces the important role of the cultural mandate in our understanding of the dynamics of race and culture in the next evangelicalism. Genesis 1:28 shapes our understanding of the cultural mandate commanded by God: "God blessed them and said to them, 'Be fruitful and increase in number; fill the earth and subdue it.'" This passage immediately follows the passage about the endowment of the *imago Dei* upon humankind, revealing a connection between being made in the image of God and the ability to mirror God through the re-creation of God's image through culture. Nancy Pearcey describes the cultural mandate in the following way:

> In Genesis, God gives what we might call the first job description: "Be fruitful and multiply and fill the earth and subdue it." The first phrase, "be fruitful and multiply," means to develop the *social* world: build families, churches, schools, cities, governments, laws. The second phrase, "subdue the earth," means to harness the *natural* world: plant crops, build bridges, design computers, compose music. This passage is sometimes called the Cultural Mandate because it tells us that our original purpose was to create cultures, build civilizations—nothing less.[12]

The cultural mandate gives humanity the impetus to reflect the image of God in the creation of culture. The creation of culture becomes a central expression of humanity and God's image and spirit at work in humanity.

The cultural mandate culminates in the image of a multicultural gathering of believers in Revelation 7:9: "After this I looked, and there before me was a great multitude that no one could count, from *every nation, tribe, people and language*, standing before the throne and in front of the Lamb." Revelation 7 speaks of a multicultural future for the church, a gathering together of various cultures for the worship of God in the fulfillment of the cultural mandate. As individuals and people created in the image of God and as people who have been given a cultural mandate, we have the capacity, and even an obligation, to bring our cultural expression of faith to the mosaic that culminates in Revelation 7.

When one culture is elevated above another, we are stating that one culture and the individuals in that culture are made more in the image of God than others. The image of Revelation 7 points to a gathering of all believers, across all races, ethnicities and cultures. The call for those who are outside of Western culture is to lift up the message of the gospel through the unique expression of the image of God and the cultural mandate found in *each* culture. Instead, we fail to fulfill our human capacity to create culture reflecting the image of God by elevating one culture over another. Do we not have a responsibility to our cultural mandate of putting forth the uniqueness of every culture and contributing to the global expression of Christianity?

EVERY CULTURE CONTRIBUTES

Andrew Walls, in *The Missionary Movement in Christian History,* attempts to describe the way different cultures interact with the gospel message through the analogy of a theater experience. "Everyone in the packed auditorium can see the stage, but no one sees the whole of it. . . . The focus varies according to [one's] place in the auditorium."[13] The great drama of the gospel message is being revealed on the stage but no one seat in the auditorium provides the complete view. In fact, part of getting the complete picture of the great drama is to converse with others who have a different angle on the performance. Simply relying on one point of view in the auditorium is an insufficient experience.

When I was a pastor in Boston, the Red Sox had a great program for clergy. They would allow pastors of local churches to attend Sox games for free as long as you accepted standing room only (SRO). When I had the chance, I loved getting into the games for free. As an SRO attendee, I could move around the stadium to see the game from nearly every angle—behind home plate, from left field, down the first base line.

Moving throughout the ballpark produced differing angles and various takes on the same game. The game itself remains the same. There is only one game being played on the field. In the same way, the gospel message remains the same. There is only one gospel message that is being revealed to us. However, we are privy to a particular angle on the gospel message, based upon our seat in the stadium.

The best scenario for watching the game would be to collect observations from all the different angles in the ballpark. In the same way that a televised game would not have one stationary camera, but instead, would have numerous camera angles, my view of the game is enhanced by moving around the stadium and experiencing different points of view throughout the park.

The best way to understand the full complexity of the gospel message is to learn from others who are seeing the story from a different angle. The necessity of mutual learning cannot be overstated. To assume that one seat in the ballpark or in the theater has a superior knowledge or perception is to fail to appreciate the value God gives to other cultures. It is the arrogance of Western, white captivity to assume that one's own cultural point of view is the be all and end all of the gospel story. Every seat has its advantages and disadvantages, and it is imperative for the entire global community of believers to learn from one another in order to more fully understand the depth of the character of God.

Practically speaking, Oscar Muriu, at the Urbana 2006 Student Mission Convention, presented an innovative proposal to further mutual learning through short-term missions. The Kenyan pastor stated that if an American church was going to send ten summer missionaries to Kenya, then they should also be willing to host ten summer missionaries *from* Kenya.[14] What an opportunity for mutual learning. The short-termers from another culture will watch from our seat in the stadium and share the differences in perception between the two cultures. Through travel, literature, film and other media, we have the opportunity to learn about another culture's point of view. Learning about and from another culture is essential in a globalized culture, and there are now more opportunities to do so then ever before. With an increasingly diverse U.S. population, it is more and more possible to develop friendships with international students and recent immigrants to learn from their cultural perspective. In this day and age, there is now no excuse to only sit in one seat in the stadium.

TRANSLATING THE MESSAGE

The hopeful image presented in Revelation 7 can begin to find expression in the twenty-first century. While an imbalanced cultural flow and a Western cultural hegemony currently exist in the world, the church can offer an alternative. Globalization means that there are more opportunities for cultural exchange and interaction. As global Christianity's demographics change, there is a need to hear from diverse voices. Indig-

enous voices need to emerge and speak into the global Christian dialogue. As in the analogy of the baseball stadium, the gospel message
must be observed, translated, and interpreted from different cultural
angles. Missiologists such as Lamin Sanneh and Andrew Walls speak to
the power of translating the gospel message into the indigenous language in order to draw out the unique cultural expressions of Christianity in specific cultural contexts.

Sanneh notices "the significant overlap between indigenous revital-
ization and the translation enterprise of mission. . . . The flowering of
Christian activity in modern Africa has taken place in ground suitably
worked by vernacular translation."[15] Sanneh argues that it is in translating the gospel message that Christianity flourishes in another culture.
"In most of these cultures, language is the intimate, articulate expression of culture, and so close are the two that the language can be said to
be synonymous with culture, which it suffuses and embodies."[16] In
other words, Christianity's success relies upon the proper translation
and contextualization of the gospel message in the receiving culture.

Andrew Walls furthers this point of view by stating that "Christian
diversity is the necessary product of the Incarnation."[17] Since the incarnation shows the translation of the divine Word into the context of the
world, the gospel message continues to go forth into various cultural
contexts and is translated into various cultures. "In Christian understanding, The Word of God can be spoken in any language under heaven.
. . . We must speak some *particular* language. For the process of translation of the Word into human life which constitutes Christian living,
there is no generalized human condition and therefore no single Christian expression. The Word has to be translated in terms of specific seg-
ments of social reality."[18] The gift of being able to translate the gospel
message results in numerous cultures reflecting the gospel message
through their own unique lenses (or seat in the stadium). The translation of the gospel, therefore, calls for an acknowledgment of the value
and worth of all cultures to be receptors of the gospel message.

Despite a dysfunctional and hegemonic globalization, which yields
an imbalanced cultural flow, there is the possibility and hope of a mu-

tual cultural flow in the church. A more global Christianity should recognize the worth and dignity of every culture. In order to break off the shackles of the Western, white captivity of the church, each culture and people group must be willing to take on the task of translating the gospel message for their own unique language and cultural context. To translate the message, therefore, becomes a reliving of the incarnation and the powerful theological work of living out the gospel message for all races and cultures. Furthermore, this translation should lead to all expressions of the gospel message being embraced by the church worldwide, recognizing that our theology and our understanding of the gospel message are incomplete until we hear from all voices.

RELEASING THE CHURCH FROM CULTURAL CAPTIVITY

In Acts 15, the Jewish elders of the Christian church gathered to discuss the Gentile problem. Around this time, Gentile believers were increasing in number within a faith that had largely operated as a subset or sect of Judaism. "The rapid progress of Gentile evangelization in Antioch and farther afield presented the more conservative Jewish believers with a problem. . . . Before long there would be more Gentile Christians than Jewish Christians in the world."[19] The changing demographics of the early church required a rethinking of how the early church was "doing" church. The church's captivity to Jewish culture had to be reconsidered. The Jerusalem Council depicted in Acts 15 serves as a pivotal moment in church history. The willingness by the leaders of the early church to release the captivity of the gospel message from Jewish culture freed Paul and others to begin to take the gospel deeper into Gentile culture. This ability to culturally translate the gospel into non-Jewish culture began the process of translating the gospel message that allowed the Christian faith to become a global phenomenon.

In the changing face of global Christianity and American evangelicalism, there is a need for leadership that recognizes that we are truly a diverse Christian community. It is not a question of needing to hear from diverse voices, it is a question of whether these voices will speak up, whether these voices will be heard at all, and also whether these voices will speak in their own voice. How do we encourage all cultures to perceive themselves as bringing a legitimate voice emerging out of their own experience and history? How can the church replicate the Jerusalem Council two thousand years later so that the church may be freed from Western, white cultural captivity in the same way it was freed from Jewish cultural captivity two thousand years ago? Can there be a hope of a wide range of voices arising out of the diversity that is currently evident in global Christianity and American evangelicalism?

During the time of apartheid in South Africa, a notable problem arose in the categorizing of Japanese businessmen. They could not be categorized as white (with all the privileges that went with that identification), but they did not want to be categorized as black or colored (with all the disadvantages and prejudice that went with that identification). Even the category of Asian was usually reserved for south Asians who also had their rights restricted. Hence, a new category was created for the Japanese businessmen: "honorary white people."

In the Western, white captivity of the church, a danger exists that all people of color will strive for "honorary white people" status. We will strive to be recognized by whites, oftentimes by mirroring or mimicking white approaches to theology and white standards of ministry. In our quest to become "honorary white people," we end up loathing the unique way that God has created us in our cultural context. This self-loathing yields a denial to the church of a fuller understanding of the gospel message from all different angles and perspectives. The challenge of the next evangelicalism is to empower the marginalized to recognize the gift that is the cultural mandate—that their culture is an expression of being made in the image of God and must be represented at the table of believers.

There is a great possibility and hope when different cultures come with their various perspectives and insights into the gospel message. There is a richness to the kingdom when the cultural mandate finds its fulfillment in the fullness of Revelation 7. In this increasingly global Christianity and an increasingly diverse American evangelicalism, the promise is of a myriad of expressions of church life that enrich and deepen the next evangelicalism. In the next section, we will examine positive examples of the next evangelicalism and the possibility of lessons learned from communities striving for the embodiment of the gospel message beyond the Western, white cultural captivity of the church.

PART THREE

Freedom from the Western, White Captivity of the Church

Suffering and Celebration

Learning from the African American and Native American Communities

OUR CHURCH HAD JUST WRAPPED UP ITS FIRST Vacation Bible
School. After a week of working with about forty-five inner-city children, about a dozen or so VBS counselors (most of them college students
or young professionals) had gathered together to reflect and pray about
the past week. During our first year of existence as a church, we had
stressed to our young congregation that our church existed not merely
to provide a comfortable place of worship for easily-distracted twentysomethings, but as a birthing ground for urban missions. To that end,
we had just completed one of our initial forays into urban ministry with
a summer VBS program for neighborhood kids. At that time, our church
was composed almost exclusively of those coming from affluent or privileged backgrounds that stressed higher education as a means of advancement. In contrast, the children of the neighborhood who participated in the VBS were coming from much less privileged backgrounds.

That fateful VBS wrap-up meeting raised some significant issues regarding the dynamics of power and privilege as they relate to racial dynamics in the American church. Laura, a sophomore at Wellesley College, spoke about her ignorance of black culture. She expressed remorse
that she had remarked to an eight-year-old Caribbean American girl

how much her hair had grown overnight. In her white, suburban up-bringing, she had never heard about weaves or extensions.

Grace, a medical researcher and a recent graduate of MIT, spoke about her conversation with a ten-year-old Haitian boy. She remarked that this child's daily concerns involved the fear of gang violence in his neighborhood and how a friend's older brother had been shot and killed in a nearby park. She remarked that when she was his age she had worried about getting the right Cabbage Patch Doll for Christmas.

Michael, a Harvard student from upstate New York, remarked that when he had asked his second-grade class about their favorite types of dogs, instead of hearing the conventional answers of poodle, collie or cocker spaniel, they replied with Doberman, pit bull and rottweiler.

These young men and women had entered a whole new world. Many of these VBS counselors had been raised in the sheltered environment of the suburbs and their previous church involvement was shaped by the Western, white captivity of the church. They were familiar with a theology arising out of the context of abundance, but unfamiliar with a theology arising out of poverty, suffering and marginalization. Because their understanding of God emerged out of affluence and privilege, their expectation of ministry in the inner city focused on how their education and wealth would serve those who had very little. Their experience of affluence and plenty had led them to assume that *they* would be the ones who would teach and the poor would be the ones who would learn. *They* would be the ones who would give and the poor would be the ones who receive. Being steeped in the Western, white captivity of the church gave them a worldview that hindered genuine mutuality and reciprocity.

When the American church looks toward an ethnically and culturally diverse future, oftentimes we believe that those who currently have the wealth, power and privilege will be the ones who will serve and lead those who are without. It is the assumption that the "haves" have much to offer while the "have-nots" have little to offer. The cultural captivity of American evangelicalism has produced a belief that material success reflects God's true blessing. Power and privilege entitle certain groups to exercise an authority over those who are without power and privilege—with the underlying assumption of superiority. Learning as defined by those with power and privilege involves instructing the poor, ethnic minorities of the ways of success by the rich majority culture. Is it possible that we are so ensconced in the Western, white captivity of the church and its corresponding value of success and power that we are unable to see the dignity and worth of the marginalized and the very least of these?

THEOLOGY OF SUFFERING AND CELEBRATION

A few years ago I was struggling to find an appropriate sermon illustration for a sermon on racial reconciliation. I stumbled across this story intended to illustrate the admonition in Romans 12:16 to "not be proud, but be willing to associate with people of low position."

> A fitting illustration of this comes from the life of Chief Justice Charles Evans Hughes. When Mr. Hughes was appointed Chief Justice of the Supreme Court of the United States, he moved to Washington and transferred his letter to a Baptist church there. . . . It was the custom in that Baptist church to have all new members come forward . . . and be introduced to the congregation. On this particular day the first to be called was a Chinese laundryman, Ah Sing. . . . He stood at the far side of the pulpit. As others were called, they took positions at the extreme opposite side. When a dozen people had gathered, Ah Sing still stood alone. Then Chief Justice Hughes was called, and he significantly stood next to the laundryman.[1]

While the chief justice was indeed acting in a noble manner, the main point of the illustration was completely off-target. The story emphasized the goodness of the Supreme Court Justice, who lowered himself to stand next to the Chinese laundryman. The application focused on how we should all lower ourselves to associate with the lowly ethnic minorities. The implication of the story was to point out how lucky the Chinese laundryman was to have a Supreme Court Justice stand next to him. In actuality, the honor also went to the Supreme Court Justice who got to stand next to one who was made in the image of God, one who struggled in life, alone and marginalized, and still sought the Lord in a church that would not reach out to him. The true honor belonged to the Supreme Court Justice.

In *Peace*, Walter Brueggemann attempts to address the difference between shalom for the haves and the have-nots: "A theology of blessing [celebration] for the well off 'haves' is very different from a theology of salvation [suffering] for the precarious 'have-nots.'"[2] The tension between the theology of celebration and the theology of suffering is the tension between the now and the not yet.[3] In the same way that a proper kingdom theology demands the intersection between the now and the not yet—a proper shalom theology dictates that there is an intersection between suffering and celebration. Ron Mitchell, in *Organic Faith*, speaks to "our tendency toward simplistic 'all good' and 'all bad' judgments."[4] In examining the seemingly polar extremes presented by Brueggemann, it is essential to reflect on how we can connect the two seemingly disparate theologies.

In *Flesh and Stone*, Richard Sennett states the central question of our striving to understand the intersection between the theology of celebration and the theology of suffering: "How will we exit from our own bodily passivity? . . . For without a disturbed sense of ourselves, what will prompt most of us—who are not heroic figures knocking on the doors of crackhouses—to turn outward toward each other, to experience the Other?"[5] How can those of us who operate under the theology of celebration connect with those who live under the theology of suffering?

MOBILITY, POWER AND THE FORMATION OF THEOLOGY

In order to bridge the gap between the haves and the have-nots, we need to understand how the theology of the haves (or the theology of celebration) is shaped by one's experience and perception of power and the application of that power. In the Western, white captivity of American evangelicalism, the acquisition of power (usually characterized by material gain both financially and numerically) becomes the means of advancement and the expression of success. Power becomes the currency of the American church and the dominant group has the greatest access to that currency. The formation of a theology based upon Western, white cultural captivity yields a theology focused on furthering and affirming the existing power paradigm. Specifically, in American culture, the ability to be mobile affects the wielding of power and furthers the Western, white captivity of the American evangelical church.

America is obsessed with mobility. We are a mobile nation that equates the ability to move with the ability to gain and express power. James Jasper, in *A Restless Nation*,[6] writes about how American-made cars tend to have names associated with movement and the pioneering spirit. Names like the Chevy Trailblazer and Venture, the Ford Explorer, Escape, Mustang and Bronco all evoke images of movement related to the wild frontier. Even one of the worst cars ever made, the Ford Pinto, is named after a horse from the wild frontier, implying the ability to do what the Pinto automobile rarely did, actually move well. Oftentimes, these exotic names belie the reality of minivans and SUVs geared toward usage by suburban soccer moms. Import cars, in contrast, use letters and numbers for their nomenclature. Even the fanciest of sports cars have alphanumeric designations: Porsche 911, BMW Z4, Jaguar XJS and Mercedes-Benz SLK. Import cars with actual names are serene and calming, such as the Honda Civic and the Accord, or perplexing, such as the Toyota Yaris and the Camry. Picture in your mind the image of the Dodge Sprinter. Now picture the image of the Porsche Boxster. Now ask yourself, which car would you have named the "Sprinter" and which car would you have named the "Boxster"?

Our obsession and significant financial commitment to modes of transportation reflect the importance of mobility to American culture. But this mobility has consequences to community life and to our perception of the world around us. "The modern individual is, above all else, a mobile human being. . . . Moving around freely diminishes sensory awareness, arousal by places or the people in those places. . . . Today, as the desire to move freely has triumphed over the sensory claims of the space through which the body moves, the modern mobile individual has suffered a kind of tactile crisis: motion has helped desensitize the body."[7] Mobility, therefore, has dulled the ability to connect with suffering. Contemporary life is characterized by movement, oftentimes at high speeds, with the absence of any real connection to the world around us. Mobility, and the speed of that mobility, result in the ability and the power to disregard and disconnect from suffering. There is no space or time for the theology of celebration to intersect with the theology of suffering—there is only motion that dulls the senses.

Our constant motion, and the high speed of that movement, heighten the dulling of our senses and the increasing disconnect with suffering. The power of spatial mobility is the power to ignore or disregard suffering. For instance, when we lived in Cambridge, our church (and my office) were only four blocks away from our home. Usually, I would walk to my office and connect with various people from my urban neighborhood community. I could see the homeless person on the corner, notice my neighbor's eight-year-old son who shouldn't be out by himself, and note that Sister Beckles may be ill because she wasn't out and about that day. All of these observations are made possible by the pace with which I walk through the neighborhood. The slow pace of walking allows me to connect with individuals and even to observe and connect with those in pain. On the other hand, on the rare occasions that I would need to take my car to work, I could take the exact same route, but by virtue of moving at thirty-five miles per hour instead of three-and-a-half miles per hour, I would fail to see a significant amount of suffering in my neighborhood. I am moving too fast to connect with individuals along my path. Everything becomes a blur as I move at higher speeds.

In the same way, movement away from dense urban space to open suburban space also heightens this sense of disconnect. Mobility allows the suburbanite to move from his living room to the garage to get into his highly treasured automobile. The car takes him from his garage to the highway on his way to the city at the highest speed possible. The fifty-five-plus-miles-per-hour movement in the comfort of one's vehicle allows the driver to escape and disconnect from a fast moving world around him. When he gets to his place of work, he can proceed directly to his building's underground parking garage and take the elevator up to his office.

During his high speed commute, he has had no opportunity to connect with anyone in the city. Instead his mobility has allowed him to see the world pass by in a blur. Mobility affords him the luxury of dwelling in the theology of celebration with no need to connect with any suffering.

Mobility is not limited to a geographic and spatial mobility but also includes an economic mobility and a technological mobility. Individuals with the power to move of their own volition will experience upward mobility. Mobility, therefore, not only disconnects us from suffering, but it also fragments American society by the unequal distribution of power based upon mobility. American culture's obsession with mobility reflects the historical association of power with mobility. Advancement related to mobility, such as the Wright Brothers' first flight, the completion of the transcontinental railroad and the first transatlantic flight are considered landmark moments in American history. The power of mobility is reflected in the promise offered in the phrase "Go west, young man." Mobility is the power to move beyond one's current situation to a much-improved situation.

Mobility by choice yields power or the eventual increase of power. When the movement of people groups is by choice, usually to pursue educational and economic opportunity, those immigrant groups (such as Europeans and East Asians) tend to succeed economically. On the other hand, forced mobility such as the kidnapping of Africans to the Americas for slave labor, the forced migration and eventual genocide of Native communities and immigration for the sake of survival (such as aspects of Mexican immigration) yields powerlessness.[8] These communities continue to struggle with social and economic injustice as a result of a forced mobility. Contrast the relative level of socio-economic uplift of the East Asian community (Chinese, Japanese and Korean immigration which occurred largely in the context of the pursuit of educational and economic gain and tends to have a higher level of per capita income) with the Southeast Asian community (Vietnamese, Cambodian, Laotian and Hmong immigration which occurred largely in the context of wartime refugees and the subsequent lower per capita income). In American society, the power to choose mobility is real power. As individuals have an opportunity to move up, they often are moving away. As highly mobile individuals, therefore, there is limited opportunity to connect with those who are held in place by a system of survival and suffering.

Furthermore, the advent of a high-tech, low-touch world is changing the way we connect to the world around us because society now moves at the speed and level of technology. In other words, our digital world, characterized by a cyber-mobility, yields a significant sense of disconnect from other individuals and from society. One example is how our current means of communication is characterized by distance and speed. The very personal and relational town hall meetings of the past have been replaced by an impersonal image of an individual on the television set—or worse yet, by anonymous reports and images that we can pick and choose off the internet. Technology allows us to express the power of mobility in our ability to disconnect from suffering. When a disturbing news report appears on the TV, we can choose technological mobility and disconnect by changing the channel. If the front page of Yahoo! or MSNBC has a disturbing story about genocide in Sudan or the famine in North Korea, it only takes the click of a mouse to move to baseball scores, which is usually much less disturbing. Technological mobility allows us to avoid pain and discomfort at all costs.

Technology provides the ultimate expression of individualism. This hyped-up individualism has created a deep sense of disconnection between individuals. "A rampant individualism separates us from one another, and yet we felt a deep longing for community and a sense of belonging. . . . Our deep need is to find a way to connect. The broken relationships must be healed; everything now depends upon our making connections."[9] Despite this hunger for community, a strident individualism coupled with a rapidly-advancing technology creates individuals who long for community but lack the sufficient tools to build that community. The power of technological mobility furthers the distance between those who dwell in celebration and those who dwell in suffering.

Disconnect caused by mobility leads to a negative perception of those who dwell in a theology of suffering by those who dwell in a theology of celebration. The assumption of power and privilege means that those in our society who have the power of mobility assume a superior position over those who do not. The evangelical church's captivity to the materialistic values of Western, white culture means that the haves assume positions of power over the have-nots. Specifically, those who have the power of mobility (i.e., middle-class, white suburbanites) assume a position of superiority and an assumption of God's blessing over and above those who lack the power of mobility (i.e., urban people of color). If the haves assume a position of privilege, the resultant dynamic is one of paternalism by those in places of celebration. However, a proper understanding of power and privilege, particularly as it relates to Christology, should lead us to the healthy intersection of celebration and suffering.

Our theology is incomplete when we have only half of the story. The power found in our mobility leads us to expect the haves to be the apex of theology. However, the powerlessness and immobility of the have-nots provides a necessary balance. We need to understand both celebration and suffering to fully grasp shalom. Our understanding of Jesus requires that we understand the suffering of Jesus (the crucifixion) as well as the celebration of Jesus (the resurrection).

In Contrast . . . the Body of Christ

Diametrically opposed to the characteristics of mobility, and a spiritual numbness and apathy arising from mobility, are the characteristics of the body of Christ. Instead of upward mobility, there is the doctrine of the incarnation. Instead of a seeking of comfort through geographic and technological mobility, there is Jesus' willingness to suffer and die on the cross. Mobility may be a high value in our contemporary culture, but the value of the kingdom of God and the example of Jesus Christ is the incarnation. The doctrine of the incarnation stands in opposition to our obsession with mobility. — *discuss*

The first chapter of the Gospel of John, in describing Jesus as the "Word," asserts in verse 1 the preexistence of Christ ("In the beginning") and consequently Jesus' deity ("and the Word was God"). Then, John asserts in verse 14 that this "Word became flesh and made his dwelling among us." God chose to dwell in human flesh, rather than moving away from us. Matthew refers to the Old Testament in relation to the incarnation. "All this took place to fulfill what the Lord had said through the prophet: 'The virgin will conceive and give birth to a son, and they will call him Immanuel (which means, 'God with us')" (Mt 1:22-23). Paul's epistles also reveal the centrality of Christ's incarnation. That Jesus "made himself nothing by taking the very nature of a servant, being made in human likeness" (Phil 2:7). "For in Christ all the fullness of the Deity lives in bodily form" (Col 2:9). As Christ chose to dwell among people and live in the flesh with all its limitations, the doctrine of incarnation would demand that the body of Christ (his church) would dwell among those enduring suffering. For example, Ray Bakke asserts that "we must flesh out the gospel by having Christians deliberately and strategically moving into the run-down neighborhoods,"[10] thereby living as the incarnate body of Christ. In order for those of us arising out of the theology of celebration to connect with the theology of suffering, we will need to embrace the full implication of the doctrine of incarnation. Just as Christ emptied himself and made his dwelling among us, we also ought to empty ourselves and make our dwelling among them.

The biblical material related to the body of Christ stands in opposition to a numbness and passivity created by mobility. Christ is not depicted as one who avoided pain, but as one who welcomed it. Jesus "humbled himself by becoming obedient to death—even death on a cross" (Phil 2:8). Echoing Isaiah 53, the apostle Peter reveals that Christ suffered willingly for humanity. "Christ suffered for you, leaving you an example, that you should follow in his steps. 'He committed no sin, and no deceit was found in his mouth.' When they hurled their insults at him, he did not retaliate; when he suffered, he made no threats. Instead, he entrusted himself to him who judges justly. 'He himself bore our sins' in his body on the cross, so that we might die to sins and live for righteousness; 'by his wounds you have been healed'" (1 Pet 2:21-24). Peter calls the body of Christ (the church) to suffer with those who suffer as the incarnate body of Christ had done. As Christ's suffering and sacrifice brought life to the Christian, the body of Christ must now suffer and sacrifice for the suffering of others. Suffering is to be embraced, not avoided. A proper understanding of *discuss*

Christology challenges us to move from a place of numbness to a place of experiencing pain and suffering.

Our theology needs to apply a total Christology to our understanding of power and privilege. Jesus' life is a reflection of both suffering and celebration. His life reflects one that yielded power for the sake of embracing suffering on the cross. This suffering, in turn, leads to a place of celebration in the resurrection. In contrast to how American society or even the evangelical church views power, we need to embrace a powerlessness that is evidenced in the life of Jesus. A proper Christology demands that we intersect the theology of the cross with the theology of the resurrection. Celebration and suffering are found together in the birth, life, death, resurrection and ascension of Jesus.

THE INTERSECTION OF TWO THEOLOGIES

The theology of celebration, which emerges out of the context of affluence and abundance, focuses on the proper management and stewardship of the abundant resources that God has provided. Because there is abundance, the world is viewed as generally good and accommodating to those who are living under the theology of celebration. Life is already healthy, complete and whole. God, therefore, takes on the role of a nurturer and caregiver and takes on more feminine attributes. In the theology of celebration, maintaining and preserving the status quo becomes a central priority. The theology of celebration is a theology of the resurrection.

The theology of suffering, on the other hand, emerges out of the context of scarcity and oppression and therefore focuses on the need for salvation and survival. Because of the reality of oppression, the world is generally considered to be evil and hostile to those who are living under the theology of suffering. Life is precarious, needing a deliverer. God, therefore, takes on the image of a warrior and conqueror and assumes more masculine attributes. In the theology of suffering, fighting injustice becomes the central priority. The theology of suffering is a theology of the cross.

The contrast between the two theologies may be illustrated in how the two worldviews might understand heaven. I remember hearing a youth group sermon at an affluent suburban church. The youth pastor was preaching about heaven and what a wonderful place it would be. He proceeded to describe huge mansions (bigger than the houses in the church's neighborhood) with big yards, a feast of good food (like steaks and lobster), and of course, video games that were beyond anything Nintendo could offer.

This sermon spurred me to think about the potentially disparate answers given by two different sixteen-year-old girls, one who lives in the context of celebration versus one who lives in the context of suffering. If you were to ask a sixteen-year-olf girl living in an affluent American suburb to describe heaven, that teenager is most likely to respond by describing a place that is a furthering or an expansion of her current world. Heaven is what she currently has in this world, just more of it. She might describe having a 60-inch HD plasma TV instead of a meager 19-inch set. She might have a top-of-the-line Mac Airbook laptop rather than her basic Dell desktop. She might imagine having a German or Italian sports car rather than a Japanese subcompact.

In contrast, the same question about heaven posed to a sixteen-year-old in Darfur, Sudan, would yield a very different response. Heaven is nothing like what her current reality looks like, but instead is the exact opposite of her present context. Heaven is a place where her parents are alive, rather than her being an orphan whose parents were killed because of their religious beliefs. Heaven is a place where she doesn't have to worry about being raped by the *janjawid*. Heaven is a place where she won't have to scrounge for every scrap of food and every sip of water. Heaven is nothing like the world she currently lives in.

To know only the theology of celebration is to know an incomplete theology. Being steeped in the theology of celebration disconnects us from the theology of suffering. When we attempt to minister out of the theology of celebration to those under a theology of suffering—we discover that the intersection between the two theologies creates an important and necessary connection. Brueggemann claims that "Jesus practices both of these"[11] theologies. Therefore, Jesus provides the example of how to cross the barrier between the theology of celebration and the theology of suffering. Understanding this intersection between the two theologies now leads us to have a new paradigm of ministry.

For those of us who have been held captive to Western, white culture, the freedom from this captivity does not come from continuing to submit to those who dwell in the theology of celebration. To learn only from those that are like us furthers the Western, white captivity of the church. In American evangelicalism, we continue to put forth leaders who have attained success by material standards. We lift up those who are the haves, believing that our church life will be complete if we emulate these models of success. Instead, if we are to be liberated from the Western, white captivity of the church, we need to begin learning the stories of the have-nots and learn from those who dwell in the theology of suffering.

THE NATIVE AMERICAN STORY OF PERSEVERANCE

Through my involvement as one of the plenary speakers at the Urbana 03 Student Mission Convention, I had the privilege of being introduced to the ministry of indigenous Christians in North America. The opportunity to develop relationships with Native Americans involved in contextualized ministry, such as Terry LeBlanc, Ray Aldred and Richard Twiss, has radically reshaped how I view Christianity in North America. Most of my early theological education was shaped by those who were entrenched in celebration, resulting in a failure to see how God is at work in all cultures. The contextualized theology arising from indigenous expressions of faith among First Nations Christians demonstrates the possibility and necessity for those who are coming from a theology of celebration to learn from those who are coming from a theology of suffering.

The expectation and assumptions about learning should now reverse direction. As Richard Twiss writes in *One Church, Many Tribes:*

> The Native community is to this day primarily viewed by Evangelicals as a needy but largely forgotten mission field, a group in need of *receiving* ministry. The flow of ministry between the Anglo and Native churches is almost always in a top-down direction, a

one-way flow of goods, services, ministry and resources from the Anglo church to the "lower" Native church.[12]

But the theology of celebration is not complete without the theology of suffering. The incomplete celebration point of view needs to hear the voices of suffering. The movement of theology needs to be mutual and flowing in both directions, not just from celebration to suffering, but also from suffering to celebration.

If any group has experienced deep suffering and injustice, it is the indigenous people groups of North America. A conservative estimate of pre-Columbus Native Americans is approximately ten to twelve million. But by 2000, only two million self-declared Native Americans lived in the United States, while another 1.3 million lived in Canada. These numbers reflect a systematic destruction of entire people groups. "Approximately 200 Native tribes have become extinct."[13] Native Americans were subjected to displacement, forced mobility and even genocide; in addition to the systematic devaluing, dismantling and destruction of their culture. Native American author Randy Woodley notes:

> Beginning about 1880 and lasting largely through World War II, thousands of Native children in the U.S. and Canada were manipulated or forced into leaving the security of their homes and families to attend government- and church-managed boarding schools. These institutions were run in strict military fashion and aimed at nothing less than turning every Indian child into a white Anglo-Saxon Protestant. Many horrific stories surfaced later from those who attended these schools during a time when their motto was "kill the Indian, save the man."[14]

The more I learn about the Native American experience, the more amazed I am there would be any remnant that would follow a faith that had essentially been used to destroy their people. I am amazed that after centuries of oppression by white Americans, there are First Nations Christians willing to engage in a dialogue of reconciliation with white Christians. Their story is a testimony to the power of grace at work in the narrative of the church. We need to hear this story and we need to become those who sit at the feet of the Native Christian to learn from their expression of faith. Richard Twiss challenges us by revealing that

> in all this time the non-Native evangelical community has yet to say to the Native American Christian community, "We need you." Why not? Because differing cultural worldviews determine how value is assigned, measured or determined, whether for a person, group or thing. The ethnocentric (based on the belief that one's own group is superior) and biased Euro-American worldview has greatly hindered the Church community's ability to see Native believers as valuable and necessary members of the Body of Christ.[15]

Western, white cultural captivity leads us to devalue a community that has experienced tremendous suffering. Our values of materialistic success and our blindness to nonwhite cultural expressions result in a theological poverty as we shut out the voices of suffering in the midst of our celebratory theology.

THE UNPAID DEBT TO THE AFRICAN AMERICAN COMMUNITY

A few years ago I was asked to be the keynote speaker at Boston College's Martin Luther King Jr. convocation service. I was greatly honored that they would ask an Asian American pastor to commemorate one of America's greatest spiritual and civic leaders. At one point in my address, I raised the seeming incongruence of an Asian American speaking at an MLK celebration. I reflected on the fact that the work of Dr. King was beneficial and impactful for all Americans—regardless of one's race or ethnicity. As an Asian American, I had directly benefited from the work of Dr. King and others in the Civil Rights movement. My graduation from several institutes of higher education, my family's ability to purchase a home in the neighborhood of our choice, my wife's freedom to work in the career of her choosing, and my children's current and future educational opportunities are all a direct result of the Civil Rights movement. At that convocation (and in subsequent settings), I acknowledged the great debt that I owed to the African American community for their sacrifice of blood, sweat and lives so that all peoples would have equal opportunity.

The American evangelical church needs to acknowledge the great debt we owe to the black church. The black church is an example of tremendous perseverance in light of tremendous suffering. The black church has been the prophetic voice and social conscience and one of the few examples of Christian groups in American history that confronted systemic injustice with the justice of the gospel. Yet, we often view the black church as outsiders to the evangelical mainstream. A recent study by the Pew Foundation that examined religious patterns of Americans separated "black" churches from "evangelical" churches. "For people outside the church (and many in it), the term *evangelical* especially means 'white.' [Studies on evangelicalism] by sociologists and political scientists . . . usually separate out nearly all of the nation's African American Protestant population (roughly 8 or 9 percent of the U.S. population), which . . . is typically pretty evangelical in theology and orientation."[16]

As the 2008 presidential election season revealed, there is an assumption by many evangelicals that an Afro-centric church does not line up theologically or sociologically with mainstream white churches. As C. Eric Lincoln and Lawrence H. Mamiya write in their landmark work on the black church:

> The prevailing American sentiment has traditionally held that the mainline white churches constitute the only relevant spiritual pulse in the nation, and that whatever is outside this narrow ambit is of little if any significance to the American religious profile. This conventional wisdom is widely reflected in seminary curricula and denominational policies to the end that misperception is compounded, and the religious experience of some 30 to 35 million African Americans is clouded in consequence.[17]

Instead of embracing and learning from African American Christians, we have chosen instead to marginalize them.

Our failure to be blessed by the stories of suffering has resulted in an incomplete theology. When we dwell exclusively in the theology of celebration, we long to experience the other in order to have a complete theology. Ironically, worship music that emerges out of the theology of celebration tends to have lyrics that express a deep longing to understand suffering. Lyrics such as

"Though I'm weak and poor, all I have is yours."
"I'm trading my sorrow . . . my sickness . . . my pain."
"Hungry, I come to you . . . Thirsty, I run to you."
"On the road marked with suffering, though there's pain in the offering."[18]

I am very aware that suffering is experienced by every culture and society. I know that almost every single American family has had to deal with the epidemic of cancer. I do not mean to disparage the very real suffering that middle-class white Americans may endure. But these lyrics do not reflect the reality of these songs being sung by affluent, upper-middle class whites. In all probability, the American evangelical who has just sung about being hungry and thirsty will have the financial resources to stop by an In-n-Out Burger on the way home from church to purchase a double/double with fries and an extra thick milkshake.

In contrast, worship music that arises out of the context of suffering in the black church reveals a deep sense of celebration. Lyrics such as

"I get joy when I think about what he's done for me."
"Woke up this morning with my mind on Jesus."
"I gotta feelin', everything's gonna be alright."
"As I look back over my life and I think things over, I can truly say I've been blessed. He brought me all the way. I've got a testimony."

Despite the suffering experienced by the African American community, the black church expresses tremendous hope.

The joy that emanates from suffering reflects great hope and inspiration expressed by the entire community. "The [African American] spiritual was the expression of the full range of life experiences garnered by the slave. . . . Through the singing of spirituals the enslaved were able to release their repressed emotions and anxieties and simultaneously experience the exhilaration of being creative under circumstances of unbelievable stress."[19] Arising out of the context of slavery, spirituals and gospel music express a profound hope and the healthy intersection of suffering and celebration. "The slaves' historical identity as a unique people was peculiarly their own. In the spirituals the slaves affirmed and reaffirmed that identity religiously as they suffered and celebrated their journey from slavery to freedom."[20]

Lessons from the black church or lessons arising out of the theology of suffering can lead to freedom from the Western, white captivity of the church. Incarnation among the suffering rather than a social-climbing mobility becomes a central expression of a church steeped in a theology of suffering. "For many black urban churches, residential segregation has meant that their locations have been relatively constant, almost to the point of permanence."[21] Because of a lack of mobility, these churches practice a more incarnational model of ministry. Furthermore, in contrast to the individualism of Western, white culture, the disenfranchised African American community has a heightened sense of need to connect relationally and operate communally. "In the Black Church, singing together . . . is the reaffirmation of a common bond that, while inviolate, has suffered the pain of separation since the last occasion of physical togetherness."[22] The black church has much to teach us, yet we often ignore the unique and positive expressions of faith in the African American community.

The most famous American Christian leader of the twentieth century is not Rick Warren, not Bill Hybels, not even Billy Graham. The most famous and significant American Christian leader of the twentieth century is Martin Luther King Jr. Dr. King provided this nation with a spiritual foundation and a prophetic call that would lead to the complete transformation of the laws and values of this nation. However, most evangelicals are slow to embrace Dr. King as a *spiritual* leader. In a seminary preaching class I began a practice sermon by invoking Dr. King's statement about eleven o'clock Sunday morning being the most segregated hour in America. After I gave my sermon to the class, one of my fellow students stated that he did not feel that it was appropriate for me to cite in a sermon someone who was of a questionable moral character. White evangelicals marginalize the African American Christian community by embracing only the stories of white Christianity and continuing to fail to acknowledge the contributions of significant black Christian leaders. The Western, white captivity of the church allows for the telling of one story, the story of the celebrating white community, while ignoring the stories of other communities of suffering.

When I was a campus minister in Cambridge, I ran into Adam Clayton Powell IV at a regional student conference. As soon as I could make out the name tag, I inappropriately blurted out: "Hey, you're not related to *the* Adam Clayton Powell, are you?" He acknowledged that he was indeed the grandson of the late pastor of the Abyssinian Baptist Church of Harlem, noted civil rights leader, and the first black Congressman from the state of New York. He also noted that this was the first time that someone had recognized his name after many years of being involved in this campus ministry group.

How does one of the most famous and recognizable names in American history go unrecognized for several years? The mostly white students in the Christian group had neither the need nor the opportunity to learn about an important aspect of American history—because it was not a history that a white American had to learn. This ignorance of non-white American history extends to other groups as well. As Harold Recinos notes: "In the United States it does not take much effort to know little about Latinos."[23] For those of us under the Western, white captivity of the church, we have the privilege and the power to disconnect from stories outside of the white community.

In order to break that captivity, there needs to be an intentional relinquishing of power and privilege. White evangelicals have the privilege of not engaging with stories outside of their experience. White evangelicals have the privilege of having their experience lifted up as the example of Christian faith. White evangelicals have the privilege of being able to see leaders of their own ethnicity dominate every conference they attend. The reality of white privilege is that very little needs to be done to maintain this position of privilege.[24] Not confronting white *Discuss* privilege is the passive acceptance of that privilege, which equates to an active embracing of that privilege. White privilege continues with even a passive acceptance of the status quo, which maintains the status of white power and dominance. To confront and alter the state of white privilege requires a proactive yielding and a purposeful laying down of power by those who are beneficiaries of white privilege.

A few years ago, I was asked to speak at Wheaton College's Mission in Focus Conference. Wheaton is an institute of higher education that epitomizes (and in many ways serves as a vanguard for) American evangelicalism. Wheaton is also a place where world evangelization and missions has been a high priority. I was greatly honored to be asked to address a Christian college with such a distinguished record of raising evangelical leaders, particularly missionaries. But I was also aware that many of the students at Wheaton did not understand the concept of white privilege, having been passive, but complicit, beneficiaries of white privilege in American evangelicalism. I began by explaining the changes in the face of global Christianity and the need for crosscultural ministry in this changing world. I closed my comments by stating that there would need to be a difference in how we approach missions emerging out of these numerous changes but also in light of white privilege.

In summary, I said, "If you are a white Christian wanting to be a missionary in this day and age, and you have never had a nonwhite mentor, then you will not be a missionary. You will be a colonialist. Instead of taking the gospel message into the world, you will take an Americanized version of the gospel." If one does not have the experience of being in places of powerlessness, even through the simple and basic example of having nonwhite mentors in their life, they have experienced the theology of celebration but have not experienced the theology of suffering. While this state of being is unfortunate under the Western, white captivity of the church, it is a completely unacceptable state for the next evangelicalism.

In response to my sermon at Wheaton College, one student created a website referencing my chapel sermon as "some insanity at Wheaton College." He proceeded to paste a picture of Karl Marx with my name under the picture. When you clicked on the picture of Marx, you heard random excerpts from my sermon with the Russian national anthem playing in the background.

In contrast, a young woman approached me at a different conference I was speaking at and referenced my talk at Wheaton College. She spoke about her increased awareness of her white privilege and her increased awareness for the need to have nonwhite mentors. She had recently joined an African American church as a member, not as a leader or as a missionary. She spoke about taking bold steps to develop crosscultural friendships and her experience of being "mentored" by nonwhite writers.

Which student do you think is better prepared for the next evangelicalism?

Holistic Evangelism

Learning from the Immigrant Church

MY FAMILY WAS GLUED TO THE TELEVISION SET. Even though it was way too late for our elementary-aged kids to be up, we all wanted to see the final results. The 2008 Beijing Olympics had captivated our family, and we were experiencing both the highs and lows of the women's individual all-around gymnastics competition. My kids loved the tumbling, my wife enjoyed the human drama, and I relished the sociological insight into American life. What was fascinating to me was how my Asian American family was chanting "USA, USA, USA" as we witnessed Moscow-born American gymnast Nastia Liukin, whose father had been a gold medalist for the former Soviet Union, face off against Shawn Johnson, a Midwesterner whose coach was born and raised in Beijing but whose training center happened to be in Iowa. All the while, Bela Karolyi, a Romanian American, was displaying histrionics while commenting on the competition from the studio. The Russian immigrant family, the Iowa teenager, the Chinese immigrant coach, the Romanian immigrant commentator and the Korean American family watching it were all part of the "USA, USA, USA."

Immigration is a fact of American life. For several centuries, peoples from far-off lands have landed upon the shores of the United States, both willingly and by force. If we really want to understand America, we must understand the immigrant story. And if we really want to understand immigrants, we must understand not only their premigration history, their economic struggles and their sociological adjustment to a new land; but most importantly, we must understand the faith of the immigrant community. Faith and the faith community provide a lifeline for the new immigrant.

In studying the immigrant church, we examine one of the most dynamic areas of church growth in the United States and get a glimpse of the next evangelicalism. In this chapter, we examine the story of one particular immigrant community to gain larger insight into the immigrant church's development in America. In effect, by focusing on the development of the Korean American immigrant church during the decades between the 1970s and the 1990s, I am telling my family's story. On a less personal level, a case study of the Korean American immigrant church points us toward a model of evangelism and church growth that arises out of a primary cultural context intersecting with a secondary society. While the focus of this chapter will be on the Korean American story, I have found that in the particularity of the Korean American immigrant church experience there are many parallels and connections to other immigrant groups.

FINDING A HOME IN AMERICA

I had just thrown up all over my new suit. After two excruciatingly long flights from Seoul to Seattle to Washington, D.C., my six-year-old body reacted during our downward descent into Dulles International Airport. Luckily, before our departure from Korea in 1973, my mom had purchased two new suits for America. So there I was, stepping off the plane and onto those unusual military transport vehicles they use at Dulles, dressed in a red blazer, white pants and a blue bow tie. Everything was new, everything was different. But we were now in the United States to stay. We were among a wave of Korean immigration to the United States in the 1970s. If you were to poll second-generation Korean Americans, they are likely to remember flying to the U.S. for the first time in the decade of the seventies.

The migration of Korean nationals to the United States, though initiated in the early part of the twentieth century,[1] is most evident from the
mid-1960s on. "The Immigration and Naturalization Act of 1965 abol-
ished the national origins quota system . . . [with the result that] the
Korean share of the total United States immigration increased from 0.7
percent to 3.8 percent."[2] Close to eight hundred thousand Koreans came
to the U.S. in the time period between 1965 and 1990. Census figures
list the 2000 Korean population in the United States at over 1.25 million.[3] The bulk of Korean immigrants in the United States, therefore,
would be recent immigrants (categorized as first-generation), within the
past forty years, or American-born Korean Americans (categorized as
second or third-generation).

To the Korean immigrant, the ethnic Christian church plays the most
significant role in his or her life and is unsurpassed in influence and
importance. Two different studies reveal that active participation in the
Korean church ranges from 70 to 77 percent of the immigrant population.[4] Attending a Korean immigrant church is assumed when you are a
Korean immigrant. Our very first social activity outside of the immediate family was to attend a Korean church the first weekend we arrived in
the United States. Everyone came up to ask questions about our trip,
what part of Seoul were we from, what neighborhood we were living in.
My dad's friend happened to be the pastor of the church and my mom
knew a few of the families from back in Korea. For the first few months
in the United States, aside from white and black Americans we saw from
a distance, the only Americans we had met and interacted with were
actually Korean. In some ways, the Korean immigrant church made it
seem like we had never left Korea.

As the Korean immigrant population increased dramatically from
the 1970s and into the 1990s, so also did the number of Korean immigrant churches. "Due to an influx of new immigrants who arrive in the
United States with their own religious preference, it is quite reasonable
to expect them to look for the church of their choice or to establish their
own denominational church. This seems to be a major cause for the
proliferation of churches."[5] "The number of Korean immigrant churches

has grown even faster than the population, from about 75 churches in 1970 to about 2,000 today [1990]. . . . This would mean that there is one Korean church for every 350 Koreans in the United States."[6] The proliferation of Korean churches is not only a result of transfer growth (i.e., Christians from Korea bringing their faith to the United States) but reflective of a holistic evangelism effort.

The Korean immigrant church has been the most influential, formative and stable institution in the Korean immigrant community, an institution that has helped to shape Korean American identity. It is evident that the power of the Holy Spirit is at work in the growth of the Korean church in the United States. The simple but true answer to what has spurred this phenomenal growth in the Korean American church is prayer and the work of God. At the same time, God's spiritual work often corresponds to a number of sociological factors that contribute to the growth of the church. God worked through various social factors to bring about revival in the Korean immigrant community. Five characteristics emerge as important elements of understanding church growth in the Korean immigrant church context:

1. worship in the heart language of the immigrant
2. maintenance of homeland culture
3. the importance of fellowship community life and social networking
4. the provision of social services
5. the restoration of social status.

LANGUAGE, CULTURE AND THE IMMIGRANT CHURCH

When my dad left our family not long after we came to the United States, our family faced tremendous turmoil, not only because we had lost our principle wage earner but also because he was the one in our family who knew how to speak English and communicate with American society. My mom was now a single parent striving to make ends meet and raise four kids in inner-city Baltimore. She worked a ten-hour shift during the day at an inner-city fast-food carryout, then proceeded to work the night shift as a nurse's aide in an urban nursing home. Her work required her to converse in a language that was unfamiliar and difficult for her. She worked nearly twenty hours a day, six days a week. She was intentional about keeping the Sabbath and maintaining Sunday as her day of worship. One day a week she could be part of a faith community that used her heart language instead of struggling with a language foreign to her in environments that took her out of her comfort zone.

The primary motivation for the establishment of a large number of Korean immigrant churches is the need for churches that minister to the immigrants in their own language. With over half of the Korean immigrant population coming from church backgrounds,[7] it would seem natural for these immigrants, who struggle with a foreign language in American society, to attend a church that ministered to them in a language that was their own. For the Korean immigrant, coping with the sociological changes caused by immigration is difficult enough; to adjust to another language in an extremely personal area of life would be an unnecessary burden.

Given the *anomie* and displacement already experienced through immigration, is it fair to ask my mom (now in her late seventies) to attend a service in a language that is not her heart language? Instead, my mom needs a church home where her faith is communicated in a language that she can understand. She needs a church that uses the language of her youth and the language with which she reads the Bible in her personal devotions. "Korean, [therefore] is used exclusively as the medium of language for religious services for adult immigrants."[8] Hence, the immigrant church becomes the haven where their heart language is the language of norm.

The Korean immigrant church not only ministers spiritual nurture in one's own language, it plays an important role in the maintenance of the homeland culture and one's identity as a Korean. Growing up in the Korean church, there were key markers for certain times of the year. To my nonimmigrant American friends, it was the new year when "Auld Lang Syne" was sung and Dick Clark pronounced that it was so. To me, it was not the new year until my mom dressed in her traditional Korean outfit *(hanbok)* and we went to church and ate rice cake soup.

There was always a lunch meal after the service on Sunday, always Korean food. I don't ever remember a tuna casserole, a cheese and cracker spread, or a string bean and fried onion side dish being served at a church function. Even if there was some turkey meat available during Thanksgiving time, it was always accompanied by rice and *kimchi*. The church is not only the haven where a familiar language is spoken, it is the haven where Korean culture and traditions are maintained.[9] The Korean immigrant may be rejected by their neighbors and coworkers for their funny accents, strange customs and smelly foods; but in the Korean immigrant church, this different behavior is accepted and promoted.

The immigrant Korean would also desire for their children to be connected with their parent's culture. I vividly remember being in a Korean church on a Saturday morning or a summer day, sitting through seemingly interminable Korean language classes. All my American friends were at home watching Saturday-morning cartoons and WWF wrestling on television, but I was stuck in the basement of my Korean church. A few years ago at a conference for Korean college students, I happened to be seated next to the individual who credentialed all of the Korean language schools in the United States. He told me that of the nearly three hundred Korean language schools in the United States at that time, only one was not meeting in a Korean church. The Korean church, therefore, is an important arena through which home language and culture are affirmed not only for the first generation but the succeeding generations as well.

The role of the Korean immigrant church in maintaining language and culture is a common phenomenon among most immigrant groups.

> Among many immigrant groups in the United States, it is commonly observed that the language used in sermons, liturgy, or hymns is often the one spoken in the homeland; that certain rites and holidays are observed which are celebrated only by members of the special ethnic group; and that quite often celebrations com-

memorate events unique to the history of the group. The ethnic church commonly has special educational programs designed to teach its youth those special loyalties necessary for the survival of the group. This frequently includes instructions in the history and language of the homeland.[10]

In the African American community, "as the only stable and coherent institutional area to emerge from slavery, black churches were not only dominant in their communities but they also became the womb of black culture and a number of major social institutions."[11] In the same way, the Korean immigrant church has been the most stable and coherent institution in the Korean community, providing cultural maintenance of native traditions. The Korean church, then, becomes not only a spiritual center, but also a center for cultural and social concerns related to language and culture. Language alone does not necessitate the formation of the Korean immigrant church, but the additional factor of cultural affirmation contributes to the proliferation of Korean immigrant churches.

But the factors of language and culture do not sufficiently explain the tremendous increase of Korean immigrant participation in the Christian church. "The increase in the proportion of Christians among Korean immigrants from approximately 50 percent in Korea to 70 percent in the United States indicates that roughly 40 percent of non-Christian Korean immigrants have become Christians since their immigration."[12] While language and culture may explain the reason why up to half of Korean immigrants are involved in Korean immigrant churches, the 40 percent increase in participation by the Korean community must be explained by other factors. Why, then, did Korean immigrant churches grow at the rate they did between the decades of the 1970s and 1990s?

IT'S NOT WHAT YOU KNOW, IT'S WHO YOU KNOW

My uncle passed away a few years ago. He died of lung cancer, surrounded by his immediate family, with scores of supporters from his local Korean church at the hospital. A few years before his death, I would have considered this scenario to be impossible. Not that my uncle would die of lung cancer (he had smoked for most of his life), but the fact that he was surrounded by friends from *church*.

My mom was the first Christian in her family. Some members of her family in Korea were Buddhist, but they were, by and large, agnostics and atheists. She made numerous efforts to witness to her siblings, but particularly to her young brother (the easiest target, since he was the only younger sibling that she had). My uncle had suffered through a number of different personal tragedies (including the death of his first wife). He was a widower with four young children in rural Korea. Eventually, he would remarry and his home life would stabilize, but he remained a staunch atheist who refused to discuss anything related to matters of faith. When he and his family immigrated to the United States for a fresh start and for his children's educational opportunities, my mom seized the opportunity. This would be the trigger to bring her younger brother to faith. So she ramped up her efforts to evangelize my uncle, but he would have none of it. The "you need to go to church because I'm your older sister" approach didn't seem to be working, so I think my mom began to scale down her initial efforts after a month or so.

Several months after he arrived in the United States, he began not only to regularly attend a local Korean church, but actively participate in the church. This change of heart occurred not because of his sister's insistence but because not being involved in a Korean church meant that he had no friends. If he wanted to go fishing on Sunday, all of his potential fishing buddies were at church. He would have to wait for the next church fishing outing to go fishing with friends. If he wanted to make a business connection, he would have to go to church to build any sort of trust relationship with another Korean businessman. When all his potential peers, friends and associates were deeply involved in the church, he needed to join a church to build any sort of social network. He quickly became involved in the church, became a deacon at the church and, I believe, experienced a genuine faith conversion.

At his funeral, I was helping out at the front table with the guest book. The guest book asked for the mourner's name, address and how they knew the deceased. A quick glance at the guest list revealed that, aside from immediate family, only five of the 150 mourners were not affiliated with my uncle's church. By the time of his passing, the social world of my uncle (the former staunch atheist who wanted nothing to do with church) was built around the Korean church.

For even the non-Christian immigrant, coming to the United States focuses his or her social network in the context of the Korean immigrant church. "A large proportion of Korean immigrant church attendants were not Christians in Korea. Many probably began attending the ethnic church primarily because it met their practical needs associated with immigrant adjustment."[13] An important element of the life of the Korean immigrant church is the fellowship and social relationships that develop at church. "For the Korean American, church was the most common place to meet their post-immigration friends."[14] New immigrants, alienated by their new and sometimes hostile environment, need a context within which they can feel the affirmation and support of their own ethnic community. "When minority groups are subjected to discrimination, they are found to develop strong kinship ties within their respective groups. These kinship ties are interpreted as a supportive structure in a somewhat hostile environment."[15] Association with fellow ethnics, therefore, is essential in dealing with alienation and discrimination.

Parallels to this sociological need can be found in the African American community. "This function of satisfying the need for primary social interactions was important particularly for Afro-Americans before emancipation, when they were completely alienated from the white society. The black church for them was the family and community center."[16] The Korean church, like the black church for the African American, is *the* social network among immigrant Koreans, where social interactions and networks are built in a foreign land.

Because of its important sociological function, church social activities in the Korean immigrant church are prevalent. "Available reports on the projects sponsored by the church in the Korean American community today seem to indicate that more emphasis is being given to recreational and social activities for group cohesion than to educational and political programs."[17] Every major holiday (even those that fall on a weekday) has a church social activity planned for it. Social events such as church picnics, bazaars, sports tournaments and retreats dominate the calendar of a Korean immigrant church.

In many ways, the Korean church operates like an extended family group. A 1989 study of Korean immigrant churches in New York[18] revealed a significant number of small churches. In New York, 59 percent of the churches have less than one hundred members (including children), while only 5.4 percent of the churches have more than five hundred members (including children). Even large churches seek to evoke a "small church feel" by implementing active home groups and cell groups, with 80 percent of New York churches having home groups. These statistics reveal a desire for intimate fellowship in a small group setting. The church becomes a place where the immigrant's desire for an extended family environment lost in immigration is fulfilled. The Korean immigrant church provides an extended family group in a seemingly hostile society.

SOCIAL SERVICES AND THE IMMIGRANT CHURCH

My cousin came to the United States under difficult circumstances. Recently widowed and a single mom of two teenaged boys, she came to the United States under the sponsorship of our family. She came hoping for more educational opportunities for her children. As a single mom in a foreign country, she needed much more help than our family could provide. Without the support of her Korean church, she and her two boys would not have survived the transition to life in the United States.

Elders at her church suggested an apartment complex where she could move her family. Not only was the rent affordable, but more importantly, other church members lived nearby to lend assistance when needed. A family at her church helped her find a part-time job in one of the businesses that the family owned. Her teenaged boys would get mentoring and nurture from the church's youth group. The church provided the support that she and her boys would so desperately need. Her sons would eventually go on to further their education—with the oldest boy now a university research professor in chemistry and the younger son an engineer for the federal government.

In addition to providing social networks and community, the Korean immigrant ethnic church also provides much needed social services for church members and the Korean community, particularly for the new and recent immigrant. "The Korean church has traditionally functioned as a 'reception center' for the newly arrived immigrants."[19] Support is consistently offered to the new immigrant through the network of the church, where established immigrants are willing to lend whatever aid and assistance is needed by the recent immigrant. "New immigrants need different kinds of information and services for the initial immigration orientation and successful adjustment in the United States. . . . The Korean ethnic church seems to be the only social institution that most immigrants turn to for useful information and services."[20]

Alienation because of language and cultural barriers compels many new immigrants to seek social service support from the Korean church rather than from existing government agencies. "Korean friends emerged as the most trusted non-kinship members in time of personal crisis. Korean ministers or priests were consulted by many respondents. However, only a small proportion of the respondents discussed their problems with American friends or colleagues at work."[21] The network of the Korean church and the efforts of the Korean church pastor are the two factors that are of great significance in the sociological adjustment of the new immigrant.

The pastor often served the dual role of spiritual leader and social worker. The immigrant church pastor was often the first line of social services. The pastor would oftentimes be the main source of English translation for the confusing amount of government paperwork received by the recent immigrant. The pastor of an immigrant church is on call for any and all social service needs in the immigrant church community.

I was having lunch with one of my friends who pastors a first-generation immigrant Brazilian church. During the hour we were at lunch, my pastor friend received at least a dozen phone calls—one almost every five minutes. He didn't answer all of the calls so I asked why he was receiving so many phone calls. He said that the last call he took was a request to have him stop by to bless a new business that was being opened by one of his congregants; another call was a request to have him come by to translate some paperwork from a government agency; and one time he had even received a phone call asking which cell phone service would be the best choice. The immigrant church and the pastor of the immigrant church play a central role in the provision of needed social services and in the social adjustment of the new immigrant to life in America.

The church provides the additional social service of dealing with family issues. The priority for most Korean churches as they grow in size is not an associate pastor for the Korean immigrant adult, but rather, the hiring of a part-time youth pastor. The church provides "child care" for immigrant families that work long hours and are unable to provide a family system. Family problems are dealt with through the institution of the church. The church pastor becomes the first resource for marital discord. The church becomes the second home for children and teenagers, the place where kids gather to prevent juvenile delinquency. Having worked as a youth pastor at a Korean church for a number of years, it is evident that the first recourse in case of family problems, particularly in regard to children, is the Korean immigrant church. The church not only provides the social service of aiding new immigrant families, it continues to provide family social services to Korean immigrant families.

Social Status and the Immigrant Church

A third sociological factor in the growth of the Korean immigrant church is the role of the church in providing social status and leadership positions for Korean adult immigrants. My father-in-law had been a white-collar professional working in middle management in Korea. He brought his family to the United States to seek medical treatment for a liver condition but stayed to pursue educational opportunities for his children. The process of immigration yielded a significant drop in social status. Formerly a white-collar professional, he oftentimes worked menial jobs. In some ways, when my wife's parents operated a kiosk serving breakfast

and lunch at a downtown market, it was the pinnacle of American economic life for this first-generation immigrant couple. But clearly, their
status had dropped significantly from their previous status in Korea.

Immigration is traumatic in many different ways. One of the most
significant traumas is the downward mobility of being part of a majority
group and having a higher social status in one's home country to being
an ignorable, invisible immigrant. The immigrant church, therefore, becomes a place where social status is restored. Leadership opportunities
for the Korean immigrant are not accessible to the Korean immigrant in
white society. You are not likely to find a recent Korean immigrant leading the local Elks Lodge or the Rotary. Their leadership development
and the replacement of lost social status occur in the Korean immigrant
church. Sociologist Pyong Gap Min notes:

> Most Korean immigrants experience downward mobility. Al-
> though many Korean immigrants achieve economic mobility
> through self-employment in small businesses, blue-collar small
> businesses do not help them enhance their social status. . . . Most
> Korean immigrants [therefore] need to find meaningful positions
> in the Korean community. They seem to meet their status needs
> mainly in the Korean ethnic church. Each Korean ethnic church
> provides a number of religious and nonreligious positions.[22]

Because the Korean church plays an important role in providing social status, a high percentage of Korean church members become leaders. Studies place the percentage of the Korean immigrant church body
holding some sort of leadership position to be as high as 32 percent.[23]

The sociological parallel is found in the African American community, where many black church leaders are also prominent political
leaders. As in the African American community, the Korean American
community looks toward its churches as the training ground for its
leaders. The church provides the venue by which ethnic leadership can
be fostered and encouraged. "Deprived of status and power in the
larger society, Afro-Americans aspired to achieve leadership in the
black church hierarchy."[24] In the same way, the highest level of leader-

ship and opportunity for leadership for the recent immigrant is found in the immigrant church.

HOLISTIC EVANGELISM

Korean immigrant churches started for language and culture-specific reasons. These reasons are tied to spiritual reasons in that Korean immigrants are seeking spiritual nurture in a church context without language and cultural barriers. The growth of the Korean immigrant church was catapulted by this longing for spiritual nurture supplemented by the sociological function of the immigrant church. The Korean immigrant church serves both a spiritual function and sociological role in meeting the immigrant's sociological need for fellowship, social service and social status.

The Korean immigrant church takes a holistic approach to evangelism and church growth. The role of the church extends beyond simply gathering on Sunday to go through the rituals of a worship service. The Korean church provides for the primary cultural needs of a displaced group. When the secondary systems of American society fail them, the Korean immigrants turn to the strong primary cultural systems available in the local Korean church. Evangelism is not simply the employing of secondary systems that creates a program to be implemented; instead, evangelism is the engagement of life on all levels—serving a community in need and providing the services that demonstrate the kingdom of God to those who may be experiencing a sense of displacement in the kingdom of this world.

Over the last decade, I have presented these findings to a number of different immigrant communities. I have found remarkable parallels among Brazilians, Haitians, Cape Verdeans, Dominicans, Cambodians, Indonesians, Ghanaians, Nigerians, Tongans—the list goes on. Immigrant churches continue to provide a place of outreach and support that is an invaluable spiritual, as well as social, contribution. Whether the new immigrant group is Sudanese, Salvadoran, Sri Lankan or Serbian, the experience of immigration and the needs of the immigrant community remain largely the same. The holistic ministry of the immigrant church, therefore, provides a model of evangelism that moves beyond a cookie-cutter, secondary-system-driven evangelism.

Oftentimes, the perception of the immigrant church by the majority culture is that of a mission field in our own backyard, in desperate need of our help. For example, the Korean immigrant church fulfills not only a sociological function for the Korean immigrant, it fulfills a sociological role for the dominant Anglo church as well. "Since racial and ethnic separatism (as expressed in the form of ethnically exclusive secular organizations) is not officially encouraged in American culture, while religious distinctiveness is, ethnic churches in the United States have provided the most convenient vehicle by which to enhance and preserve ethnic culture and identity. In short, the proliferation of Korean ethnic churches and the immigrants' extensive involvement in them are, in a way, encouraged by the host society."[25] The Korean immigrant church becomes a cultural island and a sociological haven that is not counted in mainstream Christianity.

The Korean immigrant church in the United States has been perceived as a mission field. It is the younger sister church that needs the help of the missionary-minded American church.[26] It becomes a foreign land in the midst of Anglo culture. It becomes an ethnic enclave that is as foreign as the jungles of Irian Jaya. The immigrant church becomes the perfect mission field: a lesser sister needing the support and help of the dominant group, a mission field providing success that can be boasted about within denominations, and a separated church, requiring minimal contact. The Korean immigrant church, therefore, fulfills its sociological function as an immigrant church for both the Korean immigrant community and the dominant white community.

However, in the next evangelicalism, is there a possibility of seeing the immigrant church, not as a place of need, but a church community from whom the dominant culture could learn? The release from the white captivity of the church requires the willingness by white leadership to lift up models of ministry outside of the dominant community. In our hurry to anoint the next evangelicalism that carries a white face and pedigree, are we overlooking the new face of American evangelicalism? Instead of putting forth yet another white leader in his thirties with a megachurch paradigm as the model of ministry, should we be lifting up the Haitian pastor, who drives a cab during the day, attends seminary classes at night and pastors the church on the weekend? Or the Dominican pastor who returns to the Dominican Republic on "vacation" and holds numerous evangelistic rallies and ends up planting several churches? Or the Hmong pastor that an entire community relies upon to be both the civic and spiritual leader, but whose church never grows past forty worshipers? Are we willing to acknowledge that the immigrant church that appears to be a people in need, might actually have something to teach us?

A Multicultural Worldview

Learning from the Second Generation

ABOUT TEN YEARS AGO, I WAS SPEAKING at a Korean church in a New Jersey suburb about half an hour outside of Manhattan. The Korean-speaking immigrant congregation was a thriving gathering of about two hundred adults. The church also had a second service conducted in English for about a dozen or so twentysomethings who were currently without a pastor. I was a bit surprised that this small group had stayed together for such a prolonged period of time. I asked how they had managed to survive together all these years without a pastor and existing only as a small group of worshipers. One of the members of the church was very direct and blunt. He stated, "I'm like furniture, I'm very difficult to move."

While the sentiment is notable when taken in light of loyalty to a church, it does not look toward a proactive future for the emerging second generation of immigrants. What will become of the next generation of immigrants? Will the success of the immigrant church translate to the Americanized children? Can the second generation emerge out of hiding and move into leading and serving the next evangelicalism?

Immigrant churches were started and developed on the basis of spiritual, linguistic, cultural and sociological needs (see previous chapter).

The second-generation ethnic church, however, is still in the process of forming a sharply defined identity. As the conveyor belt of immigration continues to move along, the immigrant church continues to minister to the ongoing influx of recent immigrants, while simultaneously trying to understand the needs of a growing second generation. The second generation is usually defined as the children of immigrants who were either born in the United States or raised and educated in the United States. The immigrant churches that began to flourish as a part of the wave of immigration following the changes to immigration law in 1965, is experiencing a shift from a first-generation immigrant church (defined by recent immigration and their affinity with their home country's language and culture) to a second-generation ethnic church (defined not by language and culture, but by sociological classification).

The children of immigrants, therefore, now have the capacity to move beyond their parents' original language and culture. For example, second-generation Asian Americans have been capable (in terms of language and culture) of attending white churches. However, many Asian Americans opted to remain in single-ethnic church settings, whether remaining in an English-speaking service in the immigrant church or beginning independent English-speaking churches. In recent years, there has been an increase in the number of multiethnic churches planted by second-generation immigrants. In the next evangelicalism, the second generation, with their unique ethos and strength, along with those in our churches who have crosscultural, liminal experiences, will be the ones best equipped to face the next stage of the church.

DOUBLE AND TRIPLE CONSCIOUSNESS

An important aspect of understanding the second generation is the formation of identity for the English-speaking, second-generation immigrant. The experience of the African American community provides the background for understanding identity formation for an ethnic minority in a majority culture context. W. E. B. DuBois, in *The Souls of Black Folk,* discusses the reality of "double-consciousness" experienced by African Americans. African Americans see themselves as both insiders and outsiders in American society. As DuBois writes, "It is a peculiar sensation, this double-consciousness, this sense of always looking at one's self through the eyes of others, of measuring one's soul by the tape of a world that looks on in amused contempt and pity. One ever feels his twoness—an American, a Negro; two souls, two thoughts, two unreconciled strings."[1] African Americans must deal with the reality of not being totally accepted in white society and having to behave in a certain manner in society at large, while behaving in another manner (maybe a more "natural" manner) in their own cultural setting of the black community (i.e., the black neighborhood, church, etc.).

Hispanic American theologian Eldin Villafañe found application of this concept to second-generation, English-speaking Puerto Rican Americans (with a broader application to second-generation Hispanics). He employs the phrase "triple-consciousness" to describe the feeling of second-generation Hispanic Americans.

> [The] second and third generation or "new generation" Hispanic places them often in the role of being "insiders" and "outsiders" to the dominant Anglo-White group, *but also* "insider" and "outsider" to the . . . first generation Hispanic *as well*. They are "insiders"—*totally* accepted and affirmed—only among themselves [other second and third generation Hispanics].[2]

Second-generation Latinos are able to live and work in majority culture. They have a job and friendships that require knowledge of majority white culture. But they never feel fully comfortable in majority culture—whether because the majority culture does not accept them as one of its own or because their background and experience do not fully mesh with majority white culture. Second-generation Latinos are also able to move among their parents' generation (the immigrant generation). They can attend a Spanish-speaking church and have a social network that encompasses first-generation immigrants. However, they are not fully comfortable in that first-generation culture—whether because their homeland language skills are insufficient or because they do not completely connect with a culture that is not a part of their everyday social and work life. It is in that third consciousness that second-generation Latinos are truly at home.

The concept of triple consciousness applies not only to English-speaking, second-generation Latinos but also to other second-generation immigrant communities. For example, second-generation Korean Americans do not feel completely at home in society at large. Painfully aware of being different when confronted by a society dominated by white America, the *idae*[3] must still live and adapt to white society. Second-generation Korean American Christians, therefore, may not feel completely accepted and at home in a white Christian community. *Idae* are also aware of not being completely at home in Korean society. While they may appreciate Korean food and culture, there are enough barriers, such as language and ethnic values, to hinder *idae* from feeling at home in a Korean-speaking first generation Korean immigrant church. Second-generation Korean Americans, therefore, will feel totally affirmed and accepted within the context of other like-minded second-generation Korean Americans. As Ken Fong writes in relation to Asian American identity:

> Even with a more American mindset, these Asian Americans often find themselves living at the intersection of two different worlds. In the world of the larger American society, they know that they can move about more comfortably and garner wider acceptance due to their more westernized upbringing. In a church setting, there are many who would feel more at home in a white congregation than in an Asian one that was dominated by immigrant attitudes. Or they might feel equally uncomfortable in both. But being marginal ethnics, they still have ties to their ethnic roots, ties that they have no desire to sever. In fact, many of the core traditional values of their Asian culture continue to influence their decision.[4]

Driven by this new triple-consciousness identity, *idae* will often remain in single-ethnic churches and begin to form a Korean American or an Asian American subgroup.

Connected to triple consciousness is the concept of *mestizaje* in the formation of Hispanic identity. "*Mestizaje* (from *mestizo*, 'mixed,' 'hybrid') . . . speaks of the 'new people' originating from the two or more ethnically disparate parent peoples."[5] In contrast to U.S. history, Latin American history reveals a long-term mixing of different races and people groups. This mixture creates a strong bicultural and multicultural identity for both first- and second-generation Hispanics. "The settlement patterns of the Spaniards, differing from that of the English, has produced in Hispanics, a mixed, *mestizo* race, with considerable biological contributions from Native American, and later African populations."[6] The result of *mestizaje* is a different view on race compared to the United States. Races are not segregated but instead are integrated, even in the individual. "*Mestizaje* has been described as a new, cosmic race in that it denies any racist pretence to 'pure blood,' and in integrating into one of the existing races."[7] The reality of the *mestizaje* identity among Latinos creates another level of racial awareness and crosscultural sensitivity. "While mixed race people were traditionally marginalized and despised, newer theologians see this status as uniquely privileged. *Mestizaje* allows a society to draw equally on its diverse cultural inheritances. The *mestizo* affirms both the identities received while offering something new to both."[8]

Biracial and multiracial Americans present another expression of multiple consciousness in a growing population. Our church in Cambridge was composed of a lot of single young people. Eventually, these young men and women find each other. Over a ten-year period of time, I conducted close to forty weddings. More than half of those weddings involved intercultural or interracial marriages. The number of biracial and multiracial children in the nursery was growing disproportionately to the number of single-race children.

The 2000 census reported that 2.4 percent of Americans identified with two or more racial groups. Sociologists Harris and Sim argue that "the 2000 census might well have yielded a different estimate of the size of the multiracial population had it selected an alternative, but equally plausible measure. . . . [They note that] about 12 percent of youth provide inconsistent response to nearly identical questions about race."[9]

The growing phenomenon of a biracial and multiracial population means that racial and cultural identity become more fluid. Similar to the *mestizo*, biracial and multiracial Americans have the advantage of navigating multiple racial identities, giving them insight into the next evangelicalism.

A parallel experience to triple consciousness, *mestizaje* and biracial identity is the concept of third culture. Third culture usually refers to expat children (such as the children of missionaries) who are raised in a foreign culture but are also aware of their parents' Western culture. When they return to the United States, they experience a sense of *anomie* based upon their ongoing crosscultural experience. They may look like they belong in the United States (i.e. white faces), but culturally they are still connected to the world they left behind. Third Culture Kids (TCKs) "are raised in a neither/nor world. It is neither fully the world of their parents' culture (or cultures) nor fully the world of the other culture (or cultures) in which they were raised. . . . In the process of living first in one dominant culture and then moving to another one, . . . TCKs develop their own life patterns different from those who are basically born and bred in one place. Most TCKs learn to live comfortably in this world, whether they stop to define it or not."[10] For TCKs, the experience of being an outsider and insider (even if they look like the people around them) creates a dual identity that can strengthen their crosscultural skills.

An experience of triple consciousness or third culture can provide a common link across various ethnicities. Regardless of their nation of origin, second-generation children of immigrants may share similar stories and experiences. Even if the details differ, the ethos and "feel" of those with a third culture or a triple consciousness are similar. For example, some of the best insights I have learned about ministry to Asian Americans have come from Hispanic American theologian Eldin Villafañe's writings and teachings on the second-generation Puerto Rican American experience.

One of my favorite movies is *My Big Fat Greek Wedding,* about an intercultural wedding. At the end of the movie, when the newlyweds are given a home right next to the parents' house, I thought, *Wow, that's what Korean parents would want to do*. While reading (and watching the movie) *The Namesake* by Jhumpa Lahiri, I identified with the bicultural struggles of the second-generation Indian American character. While the nation of origin and specific illustrations vary, the insights apply across the cultures. When I read a collection of short stories titled *Growing Up Latino: Reflections of Life in the United States*,[11] I resonated with the emotions of being both an insider and an outsider in one's parents' culture as well as in one's dominant culture.

As our family was building relationships with Haitian immigrant families in Boston, I identified strongly with the stories of the children. Even with a twenty-five-year age difference, I could see myself in their experience. I too remember having to explain government documents to my parents. I too remember the embarrassment of having non-Koreans coming to our house and feeling a sense of awkwardness about my culture and even the way my house smelled. I too remember the difficulties of feeling like an outsider at school because everyone at school seemed so much more "American" than me. The stories and experiences of second-generation immigrants and the sense of triple consciousness can be a unifying and connecting experience across the different cultures and ethnicities.

SECOND-GENERATION CONTRIBUTIONS TO A CHANGING CULTURE

One of the benefits and strengths of triple consciousness, *mestizaje*, biracial identity and Third Culture Kids, therefore, is the ability to straddle different cultures with a greater sensitivity. The more diverse American society becomes, the greater the need to understand the wide range of cultures. Second-generation immigrants have a triple consciousness which gives them the ability to understand and communicate more effectively across various cultures. Furthermore, second-generation immigrants have the ability to move in both primary and secondary cultural expressions. Second-generation immigrants are able to live in the primary cultural systems of their parents' culture, while adapting to the secondary cultural norms of dominant culture. It is through these bicultural experiences that the second-generation immigrant attains skills necessary in a multicultural world.

Bicultural Americans operate out of a state of liminality, a sense of inbetweenness. As Fumitaka Matsuoka describes in *Out of Silence:*

> We Asian Americans find ourselves in a liminal world that is cultural and linguistic, as well as cross-generational, in character. A liminal world is the 'place of in-betweenness.' It is at once the world of isolation and intimacy, desolation and creativity. A person in a liminal world is poised in uncertainty and ambiguity between two or more social constructs, reflecting in the soul the discords and harmonies, repulsions and attractions. One of the constructs is likely to be dominant, whether cultural or linguistic. Within such a dominant construct one strives to belong and yet finds oneself to be a peripheral member, forced to remain in the world of inbetweenness.[12]

The state of liminality is both a blessing and a curse. It can lead the liminal individual to a state of disconnectedness from all of his or her social settings or it can lead the liminal individual to be a bridge between different social settings. The liminal individual may elect to dwell on the margins or instead to choose to embrace both cultures. In a context where there are numerous cultural shifts, the experience of liminality can provide an advantage in living in a multicultural context.

Korean American author Chang Rae Lee, in his novel *Native Speaker,* develops the main character, Henry Park, as a man of two worlds. Henry Park is a second-generation Korean American man who is bilingual and bicultural. He listens carefully to how he speaks to native speaking (white) Americans.[13] He straddles both cultures (primary Korean and secondary American) and finds that he seeks to be an amiable man, who is hardly seen and who hesitates to assert himself before hearing others.[14] As a bilingual, bicultural American, Lee's character will listen before he speaks and gauge expectations in his context before engaging and interposing his point of view. The cautious, sensitive biculturalism described by Lee is the perfect postmodern prescription for the heroic triumphalism of modernity.

Furthermore, the call to listen and to gauge others before speaking and acting provides a model for multiethnic ministry and dialogue. Multiethnic ministry cannot occur without the unique skills offered by bicultural Americans. Liminality means that the bicultural, second-generation ethnic American has had the journeying experience that will prove helpful in the ongoing call to racial reconciliation and multiethnicity. Liminal Christians, therefore, should lead the next evangelicalism in addressing the challenges of multiethnicity. Instead of being captured or intimidated by Western, white cultural norms, the second-generation immigrant should be stepping up to take on the mantle of leadership. A multiethnic and postmodern world needs the journeying experience of the liminal individual.

When the church is confronting social and cultural shifts, leadership provides the key leverage point (see Acts 15 and the Jerusalem Council). To minister effectively in a changing context (the demographic shift as well as the shift from modern to postmodern), there needs to be a prioritizing of the ongoing process of leadership development. However, unlike the modernist perspective, which may focus on the inevitable triumph of the heroic individual, postmoderns see the value in the journey itself. Modernity looks at an individual's trajectory in a linear fashion rather than as a journey in progress, and events and experiences add up to culminate in an individual's ultimate success.

In the first two presidential elections of the new millennium, the Democratic Party put forth two losing candidates: Al Gore and John Kerry. Both of these candidates reflect a modernist mentality. Each presented his run for president as the inevitable culmination of his life's story, rather than presenting an attractive and coherent vision for the country. In other words, their whole life journey had been building toward becoming president of the United States. The problem with this perspective is that vision and identity were lost. Fighting in the Vietnam War became a medal of honor to be maximized for a run at the presidency. The Senate became a grooming ground for a future run at the presidency rather than a place of doing good. These candidates reflected a modern approach to leadership development, with an inevitable march toward the end goal at the expense of present reality. They were goal-oriented, heroic figures, destined for this task, and every experience along their life's journey was for the sake of a future triumph.

As a pastor of a local church near a large seminary, I had the privilege of mentoring a large number and wide range of seminary students. One of the patterns I picked up from many of the seminary students was their constant sense of the next stage of their ministry. Studying in seminary, interning with me and serving at our church was seen as the next stage of development in preparation for future ministry. Working with a large number of students often yields the sense that they believe that their ministry and real life are in the future. What's happening now is just a test run for future glory and promise. Christian self-help books harp on these themes. Using a modern trajectory of growth and development, these books push the reader to look ahead to a better future, destiny and purpose, promising that what's happening, and what has happened, is moving you eventually toward a positive direction.

More and more, however, Christians steeped in postmodernity recognize the value of the journey itself. For the second-generation children of immigrants, the liminal experience frames life in the motif of a journey. One is constantly experiencing dis-ease and change. One is constantly challenged by changing mores and values. The liminal state of the second-generation immigrant can become a positive expression of leadership in the journey from modernity to postmodernity. As American culture is now experiencing liminality, the second-generation immigrant brings the reality of a life lived in liminality and the ongoing journey of liminality.

Immigrants and Boomers

Freedom from Western, white cultural captivity requires a change in the perception of the immigrant community by the dominant culture as well as a change in self-perception by the immigrant community (particularly the second generation). A negative perception of immigrants by American society is reflected in the perspective of a Professor Samuel Huntington and a Prospect Heights Community Church (see chapter three). Immigrants are not welcomed into our nation and our church.

In April of 2007, a shocking event rocked the Unites States. A lone gunman had massacred dozens on the Virginia Tech campus. When it was first announced that the shooter was a Korean American, there was a visceral reaction on my part. It wasn't a completely rational reaction, but as a Korean American, I felt a strong sense of shame that someone that looks like me was responsible for the slaughter of innocent lives. After the initial shock and sense of shame came the frustration and anger. Why did the newscasters continue to point out that the shooter was a South Korean national when he was more American than Korean? Why is the South Korean government issuing not one, but two public apologies on behalf of an individual who was clearly more shaped by American culture than by his Korean origins? Why would anyone feel the need to lash out against the entire Asian American community and even against all immigrants for the actions of an individual?

In his blog, former presidential candidate Pat Buchanan wrote about "the dark side of diversity." In the blog entry he states:

> Almost no attention[15] has been paid to the fact that Cho Seung-Hui was not an American at all, but an immigrant, an alien . . . What was Cho doing here? How did he get in? Cho was among the 864,000 Koreans here as a result of the Immigration Act of 1965, which threw the nation's door open to the greatest invasion in history, an invasion opposed by a majority of our people. Thirty-six million, almost all from countries whose peoples have never fully assimilated in any Western country, now live in our midst. Cho was one of them.[16]

The Pat Buchanans of the world and opponents of immigration say the following: "Immigrants don't belong in our country. They are a burden and an obstacle rather than a strength. They will use up assets and resources that should be reserved only for true Americans, and they will be a drain to our nation's economy and government." Immigrants are described as "illegal," which is actually not a state of being that is possible for a human being. Actions are illegal, but human beings are not illegal. Immigrants are portrayed as a danger to the American way of life, and when an immigrant messes up, it is asserted that all the immigrant communities should be held accountable. A Western, white cultural bias yields a fear and a mistrust of the influx of nonwhite immigrants to America.

However, there needs to be a shift in how immigrants are viewed by the evangelical church. Can the church provide a countercultural model of embracing the alien and stranger among us? One approach would be to see how the influx of immigrants provides a positive benefit to the United States, and particularly to the American church. In *Immigrants and Boomers*, Dowell Myers asserts the important role that immigrants will play in the future of the United States. "The nation needs immigrants to fill our needs, not simply in today's world, where most citizens and experts have looked for their answers, but especially in tomorrow's. They are an integral part of our demographic transition."[17] On a practical level, Recinos asserts that "rather than being a social threat or a strain on public services, 'all immigrants together earn about $300 billion each year, pay over $70 billion in taxes, and use only $5.7 billion in welfare benefits."[18] Immigrants provide a practical economic benefit as well as revival for a declining American Christianity.

The shift in global Christianity has already occurred. The shift in American evangelicalism is well under way. The white churches are in significant decline. A seemingly God-ordained action in the last few decades has been the influx of immigrants to the shores of the United States to offset the decline of the white church in America. Many of these immigrant communities have provided "spiritual reinforcements" to a Christian community in the United States that had been in noticeable decline.[19] Revivals in most urban centers occurred as a result of the growth of immigrant churches. The church growth edge for urban centers is not affluent white churches, but poor, disenfranchised immigrant churches. For example, "in Boston the old declining and dying secondary faith is being replaced by the new and vital primary-culture Christianity that has been pouring into our city."[20]

The trends of a growing global Christianity and a declining white evangelicalism should not be taken as unrelated and disconnected events. The non-Western church is now seeing the spiritual needs of the West, and non-Western nations are now sending missionaries to the United States. During my time in Boston, I met several African, Asian and Latin American missionaries to the United States. These were individuals who had been commissioned by non-Western churches to bring the gospel to non-Christians in the United States. Unfortunately, because of financial constraints, most non-Western missionaries will serve churches among their own immigrant communities or among the urban poor. Culturally, the gulf between a non-Western missionary and white Americans is significant. These non-Western missionaries, therefore, have little or no effect upon the most spiritually needy population in the United States: the middle and upper-middle class, suburban white American.

However, God's wisdom and planning may have anticipated the change in American Christianity well before even we became aware of it. While non-Western missionaries to the United States have limitations on the types of neighborhoods they are able to move into and minister to, children of immigrants do not have the same limitations. God's wisdom and planning may have been at work in the changes in the immigration law in 1965 leading to an influx of immigrants for the past forty years. The change in immigration laws in 1965 saved American Christianity, rather than ruining it. The influx of immigrants has supplemented a declining white church in the United States.

Furthermore, many second-generation immigrants have experienced a social and economic uplift that means that they are able to move into middle and upper-middle class neighborhoods. As Myers concludes: "Immigrants do in fact make significant advances after twenty years of settling in. The evidence . . . shows convincingly that most gain proficiency with English, work their way out of poverty, and realize the American Dream of homeownership."[21] The second-generation immigrant, therefore, has the great potential to reach a Christian community in decline: white evangelicals. The second-generation immigrant has the potential to relate to the secondary culture of middle-class, suburban, white Americans, while possessing the primary cultural experience and the triple consciousness that embraces spirituality and faith.

As a second-generation immigrant, I have found my bicultural, liminal worldview to be invaluable. Many acknowledge that being bilingual from an early age aids in cognitive development. I have found that my bicultural upbringing allows me to emotionally connect with the angst of crosscultural and even cross-generational conflict—an experience that is also felt by white Americans. There are times I may hesitate to assert myself, but when I speak, my multicultural, liminal experiences allow me to speak with hope for the ongoing journey. At the same time, being a liminal person compels me to listen more. Similar to Chang Rae Lee's character in *Native Speaker*, I will listen and process internally more than externally. My bicultural experience has shaped my approach to leadership in the church. I pray that the *mestizo*, the children of immigrants, the biracial and multiracial individuals, the Third Culture Kids, the growing number of individuals who seek and experience a multicultural identity will be able to lead with confidence, knowing that their unique identity is truly a gift from God and a gift for the next evangelicalism.

Who will fill the leadership role of the next generation? Even as the demographics of the United States change, the second-generation progeny of immigrants are uniquely poised to serve as leaders of the next generation. In contrast to the emergent church, which only furthers the Western, white captivity of the American church, a truly new social contract is needed between the previous generation and the next generation. That next generation needs to include the second-generation immigrant in significant ways. Myers sees the sociological and economic need to connect the boomer generation with immigrants. He claims that a new social contract is needed in light of the changing demographics of American society. "It is time to rejuvenate the *intergenerational* social contract as a primary guide to solving our current problems. The new pressures of an aging society, the need to enlist support from an ethnically different younger generation, and the importance of generational investment all recommend this version of the social contract."[22] The American church can be a place of connection across the cultures and across the generations.

However, this connection and new social contract will require significant divergence from the Western, white captivity of the church. For instance, will boomer Christians be willing to leave their church legacy to those who look different from themselves? Will the boomers be willing to yield the future leadership of their church, their parachurch organizations, their denominations to a new generation of leaders that are ethnic minorities and the children of immigrants? Who will inherit the multimillion-dollar church buildings that the next generation of white Christians may not want or be able to sustain? Will these buildings become community centers, art museums and condo developments rather than being passed on to the emerging immigrant and ethnic minority communities?

With the significant demographic changes in the United States and in the American church, freedom from cultural captivity is needed to enter into a new multiethnic phase for the American church. God's plan for the United States may very well include a crucial role for second-generation immigrants. Andrew Walls raises the question: "Will the body of Christ be realized or fractured in this new [era of the church]? . . . Perhaps the African and Asian and Hispanic Christian diasporas in the West have a special significance . . . and the United States, with its large community of indigenous believers and growing Christian communities of the diasporas, may be crucial for the answer that will be given to it."[23] But will white American Christians accept this shift? Or are they too captive to Western, white captivity and unable to see the possibility of nonwhite spiritual leadership?

After seminary, I was beginning to feel the call to plant a multiethnic church in the Boston area. I began to share my thoughts with white colleagues and fellow seminary students. Back in the mid-nineties, there were very few multiethnic churches in the Boston area, but I was sensing a call to plant a multiethnic church. The response by white colleagues toward my vision was quite revealing. On one occasion, I was sharing my dream about planting a multiethnic church with a white seminary student. His response was that it would be more difficult for me as an Asian American to plant a multiethnic church versus a white

American planting a multiethnic church. He stated that most Christians will be more open to a white pastor in spiritual authority over them, rather than a nonwhite pastor. Sadly, this has often proven to be true.

On another occasion, I was sharing my vision of a multiethnic church with a white colleague who listened politely for at least half an hour. After that discussion, we were leaving his house when we ran into his pastor right outside the door. He introduced me in the following way: "This is Soong-Chan, who's a Korean American pastor who'll be starting a Korean American church in Cambridge." I was quite stunned. After a pretty specific conversation about my desire to plant a multiethnic church, I was being introduced as an ethnic immigrant church pastor. Of course, his pastor was not introduced to me as "This is my white pastor who pastors my white church." But there was this need to pigeonhole me as an ethnic minority pastor of an ethnic-specific church.

On numerous occasions, there have been assumptions about my language skills—that even English-speaking, second-generation immigrants would be ministering to others like themselves and not be able to minister crossculturally and certainly not to other whites. The next evangelicalism will require that white Christians be willing to submit to the authority and leadership of nonwhite Christians. During the 2008 presidential campaign, Barack Obama was accused by his opponents of being an Arab, a Muslim, a terrorist, unpatriotic and of not being a "real" American. My e-mail inbox was flooded with these types of accusations. The disturbing part of these smear e-mails was how many were forwarded to me by Christians. The e-mails made me cringe, in part because Christians were participating in gossiping and rumor-mongering but also because the attacks on Obama felt like attacks on me. It was as if my fellow believers in Christ were challenging my identity as an American and a Christian. I was stunned that there were so many Christians who questioned the faith of an individual whose testimony of conversion is about as evangelical as you can get. The message I heard was that Obama is not like "us" because he looks different and has a funny-sounding name. But our nation *is* changing. Young people voted in droves for Obama. The next generation understands that we are looking at not only a multiethnic future but a multiethnic present. Whether or not I agree with all of his policies, the election of President Obama says that the United States is moving toward a multiethnic reality.

As the demographics of the United States change rapidly, and the demographics of American Christianity change even more rapidly, will nonwhite leaders be accepted by American evangelicalism? White Christians need to see the value and worth of nonwhite leadership beyond the context of serving only ethnic-specific or immigrant churches. Will those under Western, white cultural captivity be willing to honor and respect the pastoral leadership of nonwhites? Will boomers and emergents and white urbanites and suburbanites be willing to attend churches that are led by pastors who look and act very differently from them?

A NEW LIFE AND A NEW HOPE

A local high school auditorium in the historically Puerto Rican neighborhood of Humboldt Park, Chicago, serves as the Sunday home of New Life Covenant Church—a church comprised largely of English-speaking, second-generation Latinos. When I arrived fifteen minutes before the 12:45 p.m. service (the fourth and final service of the day), about a hundred and fifty worshipers had gathered, waiting for the third service to let out. About fifty others were serving as greeters and working the information tables about ministry opportunities in the church. A forty-something woman was walking around asking, "Single mom? Would you like information about ministry to single moms?" The majority (80 percent) of those waiting by the door appeared to be Latinos, with a significant number of African Americans and a sprinkling of whites and Asians. Almost all of the conversations around me were in English, with a smattering of Spanish mixed in. Most everyone was casually dressed, with a handful of church members in business attire. There were many, many children milling around, with many of the children seemingly with just their moms.

Shortly after, the service began and the sanctuary filled up with close to a thousand worshipers. A worship band with five singers led the church in a mix of contemporary worship and contemporary gospel songs. The worship leader encouraged the congregation to sing joyfully, because "I'm not the only one God pulled out of a mess." An announcement from one of the associate pastors reminded the church that New Life was "a church going after hurting people and a church where hurting people will come." Aside from a reference to our *abuelas* (grandmothers) and an announcement about an upcoming National Hispanic Pastors' Conference, there was not a significant reference to Hispanic American culture. The senior pastor preached a sermon in unaccented English. A common theme throughout the service was God's heart and outreach to the hurting. A formerly Spanish-speaking, Puerto Rican church, New Life Covenant Church is among the many faces of the next evangelicalism.

"While churches from every imaginable tradition have been adding Spanish services to meet the needs of new immigrants, an increasing number of Hispanic ethnic congregations are going the other way—starting English services. It's an effort to meet the demands of the second- and third-generation Hispanics, keep families together and reach non-Latinos."[24] These churches not only have the capacity to minister to a growing number of English speaking, second-generation Latinos, but they reveal the great possibility of a multicultural church that crosses racial, ethnic, national, cultural and socioeconomic barriers. If given the chance, the second-generation immigrant community and the ethnic-minority community have the great potential to lead the next evangelicalism.

New Life Covenant Church "started small [but] entered the megachurch ranks after switching to English as its dominant language. The change at New Life Covenant church was instigated by the [senior pastor] Rev. Wilfredo DeJesus, who . . . is more comfortable preaching in English. . . . A decade after attendance hit a plateau at 150, the Assemblies of God church with outreach to drug addicts, prostitutes and gang members draws 4,000 per week to four services—three in English and one in Spanish."[25] There is no formula for the phenomenal growth of this church. They are a church that sought to be "a church for the hurting," a church that reaches out to the streets: the homeless, the drug addicts, the prostitutes. Initially composed of first generation Puerto-Rican Americans, the church made an intentional effort to be a neighborhood church, even as their neighborhood was changing around them. The church had conducted demographic studies of Humboldt Park and discovered (contrary to their initial impression) that the neighborhood was composed not just of Puerto Ricans. In fact, Humboldt Park was a very ethnically diverse community that included a wide range of Latino communities, African and African Americans, as well as Anglo and Asian neighbors.

New Life made a decision to be a church that served not only the Spanish-speaking Latino community. They decided to meet the needs of their neighborhood community, regardless of racial, ethnic and cultural background. One of the members of New Life is a white, single mom who became a Christian through one of the many (close to one hundred) outreach programs conducted by the church. She was going through a difficult stretch in her life and the church reached out and offered her a place in the emergency women's shelter operated by the church. She went through various programs to get her life back on track, including time at the Chicago Dream Center, which is a residential recovery program outside of the city. At no point did she look at the help being offered as beneath her because a largely Hispanic church was offering it. "I just needed some help," she explained. "I didn't care where it was coming from, I was just thankful for God's love being shown to me by this church." Her sense of need led her to be in a place of submission and learning from a community that is often seen as those in need of help rather than offering help.

New Life Covenant Church is trying to create a new culture—a culture of reaching out to the very least of these, regardless of color, nationality or language. Many in the congregation share stories of suffering and oppression. Despite what may be considered numerous obstacles to joyful worship, the church celebrates in the midst of suffering. They show a concern to the marginalized and draw individuals who are oftentimes powerless into the presence of God. The next evangelicalism has the potential to create a whole new cultural expression, not hindered by

Western, white cultural captivity.

As I was leaving the Sunday service, I noticed a sign for an open house right around the corner from the church. I like looking at interesting homes in the city, so I decided to pop in. The house was a new construction right around the corner from Roberto Clemente High School and around the corner from the huge metal wire Puerto Rican flag stretched out over the entire width of North Avenue. The three-bedroom, three-bathroom duplex condo was listed at $419,900. With Brazilian cherry hardwood floors, maple cabinets, granite countertops, stainless steel appliances and whirlpool tubs, the condo unit was built to accommodate the upper-middle class clientele that was beginning to move into Humboldt Park. Gentrification is not just creeping up on Humboldt Park, it is arriving in a noticeable wave. As the neighborhood changes, will New Life's ability to be a neighborhood-based church change?

New Life has been successful in reaching across numerous cultural differences, but crossing that divide has been contingent upon a ministry geared toward the powerless and the hurting. However, when the neighborhood begins to shift to those who have power, will the new residents composed of upper-middle-class white Americans be willing to attend New Life Covenant Church? Would a white American Christian be willing to lay down white privilege and enter into a place of submission to a Latino senior pastor? Or will they implore their previous church in the suburbs to start an "outreach" to the city employing the multisite model? New Life Covenant Church has much to offer for those willing to put aside their captivity to white privilege and willing to engage in a church that operates under the theology of suffering. The next evangelicalism must be led by churches like New Life, with a bicultural sensitivity and a genuine heart for those who are suffering and seeking freedom from Western, white cultural captivity.

Conclusion

WE FACE A CHALLENGING REALITY. We live under the reality of the oppression of the Western, white captivity of the church. We may claim that our version of evangelicalism is culture-free, that we are merely trying to be culturally relevant, or that we are trying to maintain the church's tradition, and thereby ultimately reject the claim of cultural captivity. But the reality of the situation is that Western, white culture dominates American culture and, in turn, dominates American evangelicalism. "Evangelicals have to a large extent been assimilated into American culture. Despite their strident criticism of American society and how it has strayed from its Christian moorings, they have thoroughly adapted to American popular culture. Instead of creating a Christian America, evangelicals have Americanized Christianity."[1]

The Western, white captivity of the American evangelical church has reached its height. However, when something reaches its height, there is no where to go but down—the seeds of its downfall are already in place. The Western, white captivity of the church must give way to the next evangelicalism. However, given the power of white captivity, will this release happen anytime soon, *before* it is too late? Will the power of white captivity continue to linger on, holding on for dear life? When reviewing the state of the twenty-first-century American evangelical church, it is easy to get discouraged. A sense of defeat and hopelessness can easily overcome Christians. Western, white captivity feels like too large of an obstacle to the next evangelicalism. The message that evangelicalism is held captive to Western, white culture is too hard to hear. The changes that are required are just too difficult.

Prepare Ye the Way

In order to throw off the shackles of Western, white cultural captivity, proactive steps need to be taken. The transition to the next evangelicalism requires a preparing of the way. Very few who have the power and privilege of white cultural captivity will be willing to yield that power in order to prepare for the next stage of the American church. There is too much at stake and too much to lose by releasing evangelicalism from Western, white captivity. This unwillingness to deal with the next evangelicalism yields an ostrich's-head-in-the-sand-like unpreparedness.

Several years ago a significant number of Korean American students entered Gordon-Conwell Theological Seminary. Many of the Korean American students noted that the school seemed ill prepared to deal with this huge influx. No preparation had been made to deal with the changing demographic of the seminary. At a gathering of Korean American students, one of the seminary administrators was asked about specific plans to deal with the influx of Korean American students. The administrator admitted: "We didn't know you guys were coming. We were caught off guard." The school was carrying on with business as usual, without recognizing that Christianity in America was beginning to change. They were not prepared for the next evangelicalism.

Pastor and author David Anderson relates a story about preparing for the next evangelicalism in a story about an all white church in Baton Rouge, Louisiana. "In years past the pastor had stated that the church wanted to be more multicultural."[2] But this call seemed out of place for a community that was all white, with no chance of change in the near future. But an unforeseen event would occur in Louisiana. A hurricane swept through their region. A hurricane named Katrina. "Before you knew it, half a million people evacuated to Baton Rouge from New Orleans. . . . This particular white church . . . had to now live out its Christianity with approximately one hundred new black strangers attending every week."[3] Would your church be ready for this type of change?

You have never heard of one of my spiritual heroes. In fact, I'm having trouble remembering what he looks like or even his name. So we'll call him "Frank." I met Frank at a pastors' conference in California. I had just presented on the demographic changes in American Christianity and he came up to talk to me afterward. He was very excited about what God was doing in the next evangelicalism, but he also had a difficult story to convey. Frank had recently left the pastorate after he had served two similar types of churches. Both churches had been overwhelmingly white congregations. But both churches were in rapidly changing neighborhoods that were becoming more multiethnic in one case and more Latino in the other.

In both of those churches, Frank felt the call to move toward a more multiethnic congregation. He presented ways for the church to prepare for their changing neighborhood. The first church in a multiethnic neighborhood graciously adapted and began the process of becoming an ethnically diverse church. When the next pastor came to the church, the church was already beginning the process of becoming one of the most diverse churches in the city—composed of fifteen different nationalities with no clear majority group.

The next church was more resistant to change. They felt that they wanted to maintain the Euro-American church identity and did not want to reach the Latino community in their region. This pastor strove to be obedient to God's call and continued to work with the church in developing a Spanish-language ministry. At the end of his time at that church, he was worn out in his attempt to be faithful to God's call. Not long after that pastor's departure, the church formed a Spanish-language congregation. That congregation would eventually grow to over three hundred members and would subsequently plant other Spanish-speaking churches in the region.

As I prayed for him that day, I felt a wave of emotions. He was a genuine hero of the faith. He had sacrificed his life and his ministry so that in the laying down of his life there would be everlasting fruit. I prayed a prayer of thanksgiving to God for such a faithful servant. And I looked him in the eyes to offer a personal thank you. The sacrifice you made gave my mom a place to worship in her own heart language. It was your sacrifice that has resulted in my serving as a minister of the gospel. It was your sacrifice that would spur my children on to be leaders and servants of the next evangelicalism. My hero won't make the cover of *Christianity Today*. He won't write a *New York Times* bestseller about his experiences, and he doesn't have a five-step program to grow your church. But I know that the words of Jesus to him on this day are: "Well done, good and faithful servant."

CONFESSION OF SIN

Western, white captivity can be overcome by confronting original sin and practicing the art of corporate confession. Corporate confession begins with awareness—the awareness of the reality of corporate sin and the racially oppressive history connected to that corporate sin. Racism and white privilege are recognized as problems not only in the world but also in the church (maybe even more of a problem). There needs to be not only the awareness of overt racism but also of covert privilege. Are we asking the questions: "Who do we gravitate toward?" "Who do we favor?" and "Who benefits?" Once this awareness occurs, those under Western, white captivity must address the shame of racism and white privilege through the act of confession. There needs to be a willingness to acknowledge corporate sin and express a public, corporate confession of sin.

A few years ago I was desperately looking for a Chinese restaurant on the north side of Chicago. We had just moved to Chicago and had yet to find a satisfying Chinese restaurant. Someone had suggested a restaurant called Mee Mah near our home. So I went online and typed in "Chinese delivery Mee Maw" (I accidently misspelled the name) and the first entry was a link to Zondervan, a noted Christian publishing company. I was a bit surprised, so I followed the link. The link led me to an excerpt from a skit book that featured a Chinese delivery person. There were a number of racially insensitive and racially offensive aspects of the skit.[4]

I had flashbacks of my experience with the Southern Baptist Convention and the Rickshaw Rally VBS curriculum.

I proceeded to e-mail the writers and the publishers. Through a number of different and sometimes difficult conversations and e-mail correspondences, the writers and the publisher of the curriculum acknowledged that not only had an individual wrong occurred, but a corporate sin had been committed. In contrast to the non-reaction and non-action a few years earlier by the publishers of the Rickshaw Rally VBS curriculum, this publisher went to great lengths to remedy the wrongs. The publisher recalled and destroyed all of the existing copies. They issued an entirely new edition with the offending section excised. A public apology was issued for a public sin. The president personally issued an apology on his blog:

> we at youth specialties really screwed up. big time. i'm ashamed and embarrassed and horrified (and fairly angry, also), and i personally beg the forgiveness of our asian american christian brothers and sisters. i write as an individual christ-follower with responsibility for the systems in our organization which allowed for this offense; and i write as a spokesperson for youth specialties, apologizing on behalf of the whole organization.[5]

There was power in the public confession of corporate sin. The excessive individualism of white captivity could have prevented the publisher from acknowledging a corporate sin committed by a system and power structure (Christian publishing) dominated by whites. However, the public confession of sin led to healing for the Asian Americans that had been wounded by the curriculum, as well as healing for the creators and publisher of the curriculum.

There was also healing for the Asian American community. In the comments following the blog posting of the apology, a number of Asian Americans expressed gratitude for the sensitive manner in which the publisher had issued the apology. The act of apology provided an opportunity for the healing of other wounds that had been inflicted. Furthermore, white Christians who saw the apology were also offered an opportunity to connect with those in pain, and experience the healing power of public confession. I also believe that healing occurred for the ones who initiated the wrong in the first place through the experience of the power of grace and forgiveness. There is power in the public confession of corporate sin.

HUMILITY AND SUBMISSION

The Western, white captivity of the church can be overcome by the humble willingness to submit to the spiritual authority of nonwhites. Will white evangelicals who have never been in a position of submission to nonwhites see this situation as an unacceptable state? Are white evangelicals willing to enter into places of submission (maybe for the first time in their lives) to those outside of their ethnic group? I don't know where I personally would be without the crosscultural mentors in my life. There have been numerous white mentors in my life, but I feel particularly blessed that God has provided me with significant mentors from the African American, Hispanic American and Native American communities. My life has been tremendously blessed by these and other crosscultural relationships where I have had the privilege of learning at the feet of wise men and women (please see acknowledgments).

Not only will the person of privilege learn by having crosscultural mentors, those mentors will also be encouraged and strengthened. I have a confession to make. I have always been intimidated by tall, white males. It was tall, white males that used to bully me in primary school. I always seem to have tall, white males in authority over my life, whether as professors or as supervisors. I can list a number of tall, white males (even Christian ones) who have bullied and intimidated me. But during the course of pastoring a multiethnic church, this insecurity and fear began to subside. In the early years of our church plant, a young man came to the church that in some ways intimidated me. He was a graduate of the Air Force Academy. He had grown up as an all-American kid on a Midwestern farm. He was a Republican. He was a tall, white male. But as Doug joined and became involved in the church, he was willing to submit to my authority as his spiritual leader.

When this tall, white, all-American Air Force pilot called me pastor, my emotional and spiritual confidence to be a pastor for all peoples increased. When he knelt to receive prayers from me, something in *me* began to change. I was no longer anxious and fearful about whether I could pastor a multiethnic church, I was actually pastoring a multiethnic church. Doug's willingness to call me pastor empowered me in ways that no degree or credential was able to do.

UNLEASH THE GOSPEL

The promise of the next evangelicalism is the fulfillment of the promises of Scripture. It will be the culmination of the biblical narrative. When God created the heavens and the earth and endowed humanity with his image (Gen 1:27), he gave us the capacity to reflect the community that is found in the Trinity. In the unity that is found in diversity, humanity can reflect the image of God. Furthermore, this image also finds expression in the cultural mandate (Gen 1:28). The cultural mandate reveals that there is value in the variety of cultures that are created by the creature made in the image of God. There is a worth afforded all cultures because of the image of God.

However, the image of God found in the individual and in human cultural expression became damaged in the Fall (Gen 3), and there is the subsequent corruption of humanity because of sin. After the Fall, the need for self-preservation led to covering up with the fig leaf. The tower of Babel was built to cover up human insecurity and fear and eventually ended up with the curse of a world divided along ethnic and cultural lines. Babylon continued the line of fallen humanity. Babylon reflected the building up of a human-centered enterprise which (like the establishment and building up of modernity) needed to fall.

The hope and promise of shalom unity (a restoration of what was lost in the tower of Babel) is given in Micah 4. Through the laying down of power, God promised the restoration of shalom community as all nations and peoples gather to worship at the mountain of the Lord. This restoration was inaugurated in the incarnation, life, crucifixion, resurrection and ascension of Jesus, who demonstrated and embodied a story of both suffering and celebration. Jesus' physical body ascended into heaven, so that the body of Christ, the church, can now live out the shalom community. Another phase of the reversing of the curse of the tower of Babel occurs in Acts 2. Not only is a single language restored through the gift of tongues, but all different nations begin to gather together to worship and serve the one true God. This community grows as a result of the self-sacrificial life of its members.

As the community expands, they are confronted with the Jewish captivity of the church. The Jerusalem Council depicted in Acts 15 releases the church from Jewish captivity and launches the church forward to continue pursuing the shalom community. The gospel goes forth into all the corners of the world, moving toward the picture of Revelation 7 when every nation, tribe, people and language will gather to worship before the throne of God. The future image of Revelation 7 reveals the fulfillment of the cultural mandate and the image of God found in the individual and its myriad of cultural expressions. The gathering of God's people reflects a place where "there will be no more death or mourning or crying or pain, for the old order of things has passed away" (Rev 21:4). A New Jerusalem is established where "the glory and honor of the nations will be brought into it" (Rev 21:26).

We live between Acts 2 and Revelation 21. The hope of the promise has been revealed in Micah 4 and Acts 2. The shalom community is made possible by the work of Jesus. But just as Micah 4 called for the laying down of power and Acts 15 demonstrates the laying down of power, the church in America must lay down its power—a power that is derived from the Western, white captivity of the church. The Holy Spirit empowers us. For release from captivity does not occur without the prompting of the Spirit. We are too weak, too power hungry, too satisfied with the status quo to challenge what has seemingly worked for us all these years. But if we are to build a shalom community in the next evangelicalism, then the Western, white captivity of the church must fall.

As stated at the beginning of this book, my intention is to bring reconciliation and renewal to the church in America—confronted with its past, concerned about its present and confused about its future. I still believe in the future of the church. It is not a hope based upon what I see in the now, but in the promise of the not yet. It is the promise that what Christians have repeatedly damaged, Christ is able to restore and to heal. It is for the church that Jesus was willing to lay down his life. It is for the church that Jesus longs to return. It is to the church that Jesus has a greater promise beyond Western, white cultural captivity.

Recommended Reading

Achebe, Chinua. *No Longer at Ease*. London: Heinemann Educational Books, 1960.

Brown, Dee. *Bury My Heart at Wounded Knee*. New York: Henry Holt, 1970.

Brueggemann, Walter. *Peace*. St. Louis: Chalice Press, 2001.

Carter, Stephen. *The Culture of Disbelief*. New York: Anchor, 1993.

Cone, James. *The Spirituals and the Blues*. Maryknoll, N.Y.: Orbis, 1972.

Dawson, John. *Healing America's Wounds*. Ventura, Calif.: Regal, 1977.

DeYoung, Curtiss Paul, Michael O. Emerson, George Yancey and Karen Chai Kim. *United by Faith*. New York: Oxford University Press, 2003.

DuBois, W. E. B. *The Souls of Black Folk*. New York: Fawcett Premier, 1968.

Emerson, Michael O., and Christian Smith. *Divided by Faith*. New York: Oxford University Press, 2000.

Escobar, Samuel. *The New Global Mission*. Downers Grove, Ill.: InterVarsity Press, 2003.

Fong, Kenneth Uyeda. *Pursuing the Pearl*. Valley Forge, Penn.: Judson Press, 1999.

Gilbreath, Edward. *Reconciliation Blues*. Downers Grove, Ill.: InterVarsity Press, 2006.

Hays, J. Daniel. *From Every People and Nation*. Downers Grove, Ill.: InterVarsity Press, 2003.

Jenkins, Philip. *The Next Christendom*. New York: Oxford University Press, 2002.

Kyle, Richard. *Evangelicalism: An Americanized Christianity*. New Brunswick, N.J.: Transaction Publishers, 2006.

Lee, Chang-Rae. *Native Speaker*. New York: Riverhead, 1995.

Lincoln, C. Eric, and Lawrence H. Mamiya. *The Black Church in the African*

American Experience. Durham, N.C.: Duke University Press, 1990.

Lopez, Ian Haney. *White by Law: The Legal Construction of Race—Revised and Updated*. New York: New York University Press, 2006.

Metzger, Paul Louis. *Consuming Jesus*. Grand Rapids: Eerdmans, 2007.

Nash, Peter T. *Reading Race, Reading the Bible*. Minneapolis: Fortress, 2003.

Olson, David T. *The American Church in Crisis*. Grand Rapids: Zondervan, 2008.

Perkins, Spencer, and Chris Rice. *More Than Equals*. Downers Grove, Ill.: InterVarsity Press, 1993.

Raboteau, Albert J. *Slave Religion: The "Invisible Institution" in the Antebellum South*. New York: Oxford University Press, 1978.

Rothenberg, Paula. *White Privilege*. New York: Worth Publishers, 2002.

Said, Edward. *Orientalism*. New York: Vintage, 1978.

Stark, Rodney. *The Rise of Christianity*. Princeton, N.J.: Princeton University Press, 1996.

Tatum, Beverly Daniel. *Why Are All the Black Kids Sitting Together in the Cafeteria?* New York: BasicBooks, 1997.

Tokunaga, Paul. *Invitation to Lead*. Downers Grove, Ill.: InterVarsity Press, 2003.

Twiss, Richard. *One Church, Many Tribes*. Ventura, Calif.: Regal, 2000.

Villafañe, Eldin. *The Liberating Spirit*. Grand Rapids: Eerdmans, 1993.

Volf, Miroslav. *Exclusion and Embrace*. Nashville: Abingdon, 1996.

Wallis, Jim. *Faith Works*. Berkeley, Calif.: PageMill Press, 2000.

Walls, Andrew. *The Missionary Movement in Christian History*. Maryknoll, N.Y.: Orbis, 1996.

Warner, R. Stephen, and Judith G. Wittner, eds. *Gatherings in Diaspora*. Philadelphia: Temple University Press, 1998.

West, Cornel. *Race Matters*. New York: Vintage, 1993.

Woodley, Randy. *Living in Color*. Downers Grove, Ill.: InterVarsity Press, 2001.

Wu, Frank. *Yellow*. New York: BasicBooks, 2002.

Notes

Introduction

[1]David T. Olson, *The American Church in Crisis* (Grand Rapids: Zondervan, 2008), pp. 16, 185.

[2]In *A New Religious America*, Diana Eck posited that immigration and increasing diversity have yielded an increasingly religiously pluralistic America becoming less and less Christian. However, R. Stephen Warner has countered that America remains a Christian nation because of immigration and increasing diversity. See Diana L. Eck, *A New Religious America: How a "Christian Country" Has Become the World's Most Religiously Diverse Nation* (New York: HarperSanFrancisco, 2001), and R. Stephen Warner, "Coming to America: Immigrants and the Faith They Bring," *Christian Century* 121 (February 10, 2004). See also R. Stephen Warner and Judith G. Wittner, eds., *Gatherings in Diaspora* (Philadelphia: Temple University Press, 1998), and Philip Jenkins, *The Next Christendom* (New York: Oxford University Press, 2002), pp. 100-105.

[3]Jenkins, *Next Christendom*, p. 2.

[4]Philip Jenkins, "The Next Christianity," *The Atlantic* (October 2002) <http://www.theatlantic.com/doc/200210/jenkins>.

[5]Todd M. Johnson, "Christianity in Global Context: Trends and Statistics" (Pew Forum on Religion and Public Life) <http://pewforum.org/events/051805/global-christianity.pdf>. See also David B. Barrett, George T. Kurian and Todd M. Johnson, *World Christian Encyclopedia,* 2nd ed. (New York: Oxford University Press, 2001).

[6]Some helpful books on this topic include the above mentioned Philip Jenkins, *The Next Christendom*; Philip Jenkins, *The New Faces of Christianity* (New York: Oxford University Press, 2006); Lamin Sanneh, *The Changing Face of Christianity* (New York: Oxford University Press, 2005); and Andrew Walls, *The Missionary Movement in Christian History* (MaryKnoll, N.Y.: Orbis, 1996).

[7]Jeffrey Passel and D'Vera Cohn, "Immigration to Play Lead Role in Future U.S. Growth," July 1, 2008 <pewresearch.org/pubs/729/united-states-population-projections>. See also <www.census.gov/Press-Release/www/releases/archives/population/012496.html>.

[8]See "An Older and More Diverse Nation by Midcentury," August 14, 2008 <www.census.gov/Press-Release/www/releases/archives/population/012496.html>.

[9]Warner, "Coming to America," p. 20.

[10]Olson, *American Church*, p. 38.

[11]Rudy Mitchell, "The Changing Shape of Boston's Church Community," *New England's Book of Acts* (Boston: Emmanuel Gospel Center, 2007), p. 10.

[12]Brian Corcoran, "The Growing Edge of Boston's Church Community," *New England's Book of Acts* (Boston: Emmanuel Gospel Center, 2007), p. 11.

[13]Ibid., p. 12.

[14]See Olson, *American Church,* pp. 72-78.

[15]David Van Biema, Cathy Booth-Thomas, Massimo Calabresi, John F. Dickerson, John Cloud, Rebecca Winters and Sonja Steptoe, "The 25 Most Influential Evangelicals in America," *Time*, February 7, 2005. T. D. Jakes and Luis Cortes were the only nonwhites who made the list.

[16]Edith Blumhofer, "Houses of Worship: The New Evangelicals," *Wall Street Journal* (Eastern Edition), February 18, 2005, p. W.13.

[17]This data is from the ATS Institutional Database, which is a repository of data collected from graduate theological institutions in North America that are members of The Association of Theological Schools in the United States and Canada.

[18]See "Racial Issues in the CCCU Faculty" (Council of Christian Colleges and Universities) <www.cccu.org/professional_development/resource_library/racial_issues_in_the_cccu_faculty>. See also D. John Lee, ed., *Ethnic-Minorities and Evangelical Christian Colleges* (Lanham, Md.: University Press of America, 1991).

[19]See <chronicle.com/premium/stats/race/2007/index.php?sort=SortName>.

[20]Martin Luther, *The Babylonian Captivity of the Church*, trans. A. T. W. Steinhaeuser, *Three Treatises* (Philadelphia: Muhlenberg, 1947).

[21]R. C. Sproul, "The Pelagian Captivity of the Church," *Modern Reformation* 10, no. 3 (May/June 2001).

[22]See Nancy Pearcey, *Total Truth: Liberating Christianity from Its Cultural Captivity* (Wheaton, Ill.: Crossway, 2005); Gibson Winter, *The Suburban Captivity of the Churches* (Garden City, N.J.: Doubleday, 1961); and Cornel West, *Democracy Matters* (New York: Penguin, 2004).

[23]Richard Sennett, *Flesh and Stone* (New York: W. W. Norton, 1994), p. 374.

Chapter 1: Individualism

[1]Richard Osborne, *Philosophy for Beginners* (New York: Writers and Readers, 1992).

[2]Alexis de Tocqueville, *Democracy in America* (New York: New American Library, 1956).

[3]Herbert J. Gans, *Middle American Individualism* (New York: Oxford University Press, 1991), p. 1.

[4]George Marsden, *Fundamentalism and American Culture* (New York: Oxford University Press, 2006), p. 224.

[5]Paul Louis Metzger, *Consuming Jesus* (Grand Rapids: Eerdmans, 2007), p. 16.

[6]Ibid., p. 55.

[7]John Joseph Owens, *Analytical Key to the Old Testament*, vol. 4, *Isaiah-Malachi* (Grand Rapids: Baker, 1992), p. 327. See also J. A. Thompson, *The Book of Jeremiah*, New International Commentary on the Old Testament (Grand Rapids: Eerdmans, 1980), pp. 542-48.

[8]Christopher Lasch, *The Culture of Narcissism* (New York: W. W. Norton, 1979), p. 7.

[9]Robert D. Putnam, *Bowling Alone* (New York: Simon & Schuster, 2000), p. 37.

[10]Ibid., p. 112.

[11]Robert N. Bellah, Richard Madsen, William M. Sullivan, Ann Swidler and Steven M. Tipton, *Habits of the Heart* (Berkeley: University of California Press, 1985), p. xvii.

[12]Richard Sennett, *The Fall of Public Man* (New York: W. W. Norton, 1992), p. 4.

[13]See Larry Crabb, *Connecting* (Nashville: Word, 1997) and *Becoming a True Spiritual Community* (Nashville: Thomas Nelson, 2007); and Larry Crabb and Eugene Peterson, *The Safest Place on Earth* (Nashville: Thomas Nelson, 1999).

[14]Crabb, *Connecting*, p. xii.

[15]Andrew Delbanco, *The Death of Satan: How Americans Have Lost the Sense of Evil* (New York: Farrar, Straus and Giroux, 1995).

[16]Metzger, *Consuming Jesus*, pp. 61-62.

[17]Richard Kyle, *Evangelicalism: An Americanized Christianity* (New Brunswick, N.J.: Transaction, 2006), p. 314.

[18]See H. Richard Niebuhr, *Christ and Culture* (New York: Harper & Row, 1951), p. 196.

[19]Michael O. Emerson and Christian Smith, *Divided by Faith* (New York: Oxford University Press, 2000), pp. 76-77.

[20]Ibid., p. 78.

Chapter 2: Consumerism and Materialism

[1]Excerpts are taken from President George W. Bush's various speeches and addresses following 9/11. See the White House website and thefollowing references: <www.quotedb.com/speeches/9-11-address-to-the-nation>; <www.september11 news.com/PresidentBushAtlanta.htm>; <www.whitehouse.gov/news/releases/ 2006/12/20061220-1.html>; <www.whitehouse.gov/news/releases/2001/09/ 20010920-8.html>.

[2]John de Graff, David Wann and Thomas H. Naylor, *Affluenza* (San Francisco: Berrett Koehler, 2002), pp. 2, 3.

[3]Ibid., p. 70.

[4]Richard Kyle, *Evangelicalism: An Americanized Christianity* (New Brunswick, N.J.: Transaction, 2006), p. 314.

[5]Kristen Scharold, "Campus Capitalism," *Christianity Today*, September 17, 2007 <www.christianitytoday.com/ct/2007/october/8.19.html>.

[6]Berny Morson, "Firing of prof at Colorado Christian puts focus on Christ and capitalism," *Rocky Mountain News*, August 31, 2007 <www.rockymountainnews .com/news/2007/aug/13/firing-of-prof-at-colorado-christian-puts-focus/>.

[7]Ibid.

[8]Kyle, *Evangelicalism*, p. 66.

[9]Ibid., p. 314.

[10]George Marsden, *Fundamentalism and American Culture* (New York: Oxford University Press, 2006), p. 254.

[11]Ira G. Zepp Jr., *The New Religious Image of Urban America: The Shopping Mall as Ceremonial Center* (Boulder: University Press of Colorado, 1997), p. 4.

[12]Ibid., pp. 4, 10.

[13]Paul Louis Metzger, *Consuming Jesus* (Grand Rapids: Eerdmans, 2007), pp. 9-10.

[14]Michael Phillips, "In Swaziland, U.S. Preacher Sees His Dream Vanish," *The Wall Street Journal Online*, December 19, 2005 <online.wsj.com/article_email/

SB113495910699726095-lMyQjAxMDE1MzE0OTkxNTk5Wj.html>.

[15]Ibid.

[16]Ibid.

[17]Douglas Stuart, *Hosea-Jonah* (Waco, Tex.: Word, 1987), p. 283.

[18]Richard S. Cripps, *A Critical and Exegetical Commentary on the Book of Amos* (London: SPCK, 1969), p. 6.

[19]John Bright, *A History of Israel* (Philadelphia: Westminster Press, 1981), p. 266.

[20]James V. Brownson, Inagrace Dietterich, Barry Harvey and Charles West, *Storm Front: The Good News of God* (Grand Rapids: Eerdmans, 2003), p. 31.

[21]Metzger, *Consuming Jesus*, p. 85.

[22]In *The Purpose Driven Church* (Grand Rapids: Zondervan, 1995), Rick Warren refers to "Unchurched Harry" as the type of person the church is trying to reach. This person is pictured as a golf-playing, cell-phone-using, suburban, white male.

[23]Manya A. Brachear, "A Business Model for Saving Souls," *Chicago Tribune*, November 24, 2007.

[24]Bob Burney, "A shocking 'confession' from Willow Creek Community Church," *Crosswalk.com*, October 30, 2007 <http://www.crosswalk.com/pastors/11558438>.

Chapter 3: Racism

[1]For more details on the offensive aspects of the Rickshaw Rally Vacation Bible School, see <www.geocities.com/reconsideringrickshawrally/>.

[2]For the Southern Baptist Church and Lifeway Publication's response, see <www.floridabaptistwitness.com/1912.article>.

[3]Ian Haney Lopez, *White by Law: The Legal Construction of Race*, rev. and updated (New York: New York University Press, 2006), p. xxi.

[4]Audrey Smedley, *Race in North America: Origin and Evolution of a Worldview*, 3rd ed. (Boulder, Colo.: Westview, 2007), p. xi.

[5]J. Daniel Hays, *From Every People and Nation* (Downers Grove, Ill.: InterVarsity Press, 2003), p. 29 n. 8.

[6]Ibid., pp. 28-29.

[7]Theodore Allen, *The Invention of the White Race*, vol. 1, *Racial Oppression and Social Order* (New York: Verso, 1994), p. 3.

[8]James Oliver Horton and Lois E. Horton, *Slavery and the Making of America* (New York: Oxford University Press, 2005), p. 29.

[9]Jenell Williams Paris, "Race: Critical Thinking and Transformative Possibili-

ties," in *This Side of Heaven: Race, Ethnicity, and Christian Faith*, ed. Robert J. Priest and Alvaro L. Nieves (New York: Oxford University Press, 2007), pp. 21-22.

[10]Ivan Hannaford, *Race: The History of an Idea in the West* (Baltimore: Johns Hopkins University Press, 1996), p. 6.

[11]Lopez, *White by Law*, p. 4.

[12]Ibid., pp. 4, 5.

[13]Ibid., p. 7.

[14]John Dawson, *Healing America's Wounds* (Ventura, Calif.: Regal, 1977), p. 23.

[15]Ibid., pp. 80-81.

[16]Ibid., p. 30.

[17]Paula Rothenberg, *White Privilege* (New York: Worth, 2002), p. 1.

[18]Richard Dyer, "The Matter of Whiteness in White Privilege," in Rothenberg, *White Privilege*, p. 11.

[19]Ibid., p. 12.

[20]Virgilio Elizondo, *Galilean Journey: The Mexican-American Promise* (Maryknoll, N.Y.: Orbis, 1983), p. 25.

[21]Peggy McIntosh, "Unpacking the Invisible Knapsack," in Rothenberg, *White Privilege*, pp. 97-101; Numerous online versions of the article can be found, see <www.nymbp.org/reference/WhitePrivilege.pdf>.

[22]Rothenberg, *White Privilege*, p. 2.

[23]Samuel Huntington, *Who Are We?* (New York: Simon & Schuster, 2004), p. 18.

[24]Ibid., p. 19.

[25]Ibid., p. 4.

[26]Andrew Wang, "Racial Bias Alleged in Prospect Heights," *Chicago Tribune*, December 21, 2007, p. 17.

[27]Ibid.

[28]"Two Congregations Consider Joining Ministry Efforts," The Evangelical Covenant Church (April 18, 2007) <www.covchurch.org/cov/news/item5525>.

[29]Ibid.

[30]Peter T. Nash, *Reading Race, Reading the Bible* (Minneapolis: Fortress, 2003), p. 58.

[31]Ibid., pp. 25, 26.

[32]Edward Said, *Orientalism* (New York: Vintage, 1978), p. 3.

[33]Ibid.

[34]Austin Chee, "A Public Apology to Our Asian American Brothers and Sisters," online posting (March 14, 2007) YSMARKO <www.ysmarko.com/?p=1379>.

[35]Charles Hodge, *Systematic Theology* (New York: Scribner, Armstrong, 1986), 2:96.

[36]Ibid., 2:99.

[37]George Kelsey, *Racism and the Christian Understanding of Man* (New York: Scribner's, 1965), pp. 73, 27, 145.

[38]Karl Barth, *Church Dogmatics* 3/1, ed. G. W. Bromiley and T. F. Torrance, trans. O. Bussey, J. W. Edwards and Harold Knight (Edinburgh: T & T Clark, 1958), p. 186.

[39]Anthony Hoekema, *Created in God's Image* (Grand Rapids: Eerdmans, 1986), p. 13.

[40]Barth, *Church Dogmatics,* p. 186.

[41]Thomas Maston, *The Bible and Race* (Nashville: Broadman, 1959), p. 12.

[42]Emil Brunner, *Man in Revolt* (Philadelphia: Westminster Press, 1939), p. 140.

[43]Kelsey, *Racism,* p. 23.

[44]Maston, *Bible and Race,* p. 10.

[45]Ibid., p. 117.

[46]Bill Hybels, "Harder Than Anyone Can Imagine," *Christianity Today,* April 2005, p. 38.

[47]Curtiss Paul DeYoung, Michael O. Emerson, George Yancey and Karen Chai Kim, *United by Faith* (New York: Oxford University Press, 2003), p. 131.

[48]Ibid., p. 1.

[49]Ibid., p. 2.

[50]Ibid.

[51]See William E. Kratt, "Diversity in Evangelical Christian Higher Education" (Ph.D. diss., Claremont Graduate University, 2004), pp. 13-14. Kratt uses the term "traditional/conservative" to describe an "approach to multiculturalism [that] emphasizes one-way assimilation of fading minority identities into dominant cultural beliefs and values" versus the "moderate/liberal view" where emphasis is placed on valuing and appreciating cultural differences. I extend Kratt's perspective by stating that the "traditional/conservative" view reflects a supposed color-blindness that tends to favor majority culture and that the "moderate/liberal" view of appreciating cultural differences is not possible without racial reconciliation.

Chapter 4: The Church Growth Movement and Megachurches

[1]See Gary McIntosh, "Why Church Growth Can't Be Ignored," in *Evaluating the Church Growth Movement: Five Views* (Grand Rapids: Zondervan, 2004), pp. 7-28.

[2]Ibid., pp. 15-16.

[3]Bill Bishop, *The Big Sort* (New York: Houghton Mifflin, 2008), p. 159.

[4]David Moberg, *The Great Reversal* (New York: J. B. Lippincott, 1972), pp. 25-26.

[5]Robert Linthicum, *City of God, City of Satan* (Grand Rapids: Zondervan, 1991), p. 292.

[6]See Doug Hall and Judy Hall, *A Culture of Hope* (unpublished manuscript).

[7]The use of the terms *primary* and *secondary* does not imply a value statement. *Primary* is used to reflect the first level of relationships versus a second level of relationships beyond the primary.

[8]Ferdinand Tonnies, *Community and Society,* trans. Charles P. Loomis (Mineola, N.Y.: Dover, 1887), p. 14.

[9]Charles Horton Cooley, *Social Organization: A Study of the Larger Mind* (New York: Scribner's, 1909), p. 25.

[10]Hall and Hall, *Culture of Hope*, p. 127.

[11]Harvey Cox, *The Secular City* (New York: MacMillan, 1965), p. 10.

[12]Ibid., p. 41.

[13]Hall and Hall, *Culture of Hope*, p. 130.

[14]Tonnies, *Community and Society*, p. 65.

[15]Hall and Hall, *Culture of Hope*, pp. 122-39.

[16]John Micklethwait, "In God's Name: A Special Report on Religion and Public Life," *The Economist*, November 3, 2007, p. 8.

[17]Chinua Achebe, *No Longer at Ease* (London: Heinemann Educational, 1960).

[18]Rodney Stark, *The Rise of Christianity* (Princeton, N.J.: HarperCollins, 1996), pp. 5-7.

[19]Ibid., pp. 18, 82-87, 160-61.

[20]Nils Lund, *Chiasmus in the New Testament* (Peabody, Mass.: Hendrickson, 1942), pp. 40-41. Lund posits that "the centre is always the turning point" (p. 40). See also Lund's assertion that *chiastic* structures hold a similar function to Hebrew parallelism. If *chiastic* structures follow the function of inverted parallelism, then the chiastic structure points from outward toward the center (p. 37).

Chapter 5: The Emergent Church's Captivity to Western, White Culture

[1]Jana Riess, "What Do Publishers Mean By 'Emergent'?" *Publishers Weekly*, March 12, 2008 <www.publishersweekly.com/article/CA6540345.html?nid=2287>.

[2]Ryan K. Bolger and Eddie Gibbs, *Emerging Churches* (Grand Rapids: Baker Academic, 2005), p. 331.

[3]The website <www.kamr.org> (Korean American Ministry Resources) tracks the number of English-speaking churches in the Korean community. The website listed two hundred churches that hold a service in English, with an additional 393 churches holding services in both Korean and in English. Furthermore, a different website (<aacp.wetpaint.com/>) that tracks new church plants among the Asian American English-speaking community noted that over a hundred new churches had been planted in a ten-year time period between 1998 and 2008.

[4]Stanley Grenz, *A Primer on Postmodernism* (Grand Rapids: Eerdmans, 1995), p. 12.

[5]Andre Daley, "Racial Constantinianism and why Andre is post-Emergent," as cited in <www.postmodernnegro.com/>.

[6]See Bolger and Gibbs, *Emerging Churches*; Grenz, *Primer*; Jimmy Long, *Emerging Hope* (Downers Grove, Ill.: InterVarsity Press, 2004); Leonard Sweet, *Post-Modern Pilgrims* (Nashville: Broadman and Holman, 2000); Robert Webber, *The Younger Evangelicals* (Grand Rapids: Baker, 2002).

[7]J. Richard Middleton and Brian J. Walsh, *Truth Is Stranger Than It Used to Be* (Downers Grove, Ill.: InterVarsity Press, 1995), p. 71.

[8]Jean-François Lyotard, "The Postmodern Condition," reproduced in Michael Drolet, *The Postmodernism Reader* (New York: Routledge, 2004), pp. 123-46, quote on p. 123.

[9]Grenz, *Primer*, p. 45.

[10]Webber, *Younger Evangelicals*, p. 51.

[11]Grenz, *Primer*, p. 14.

[12]Kevin J. Vanhoozer, ed., *The Cambridge Companion to Postmodern Theology* (Cambridge: Cambridge University Press, 2003), p. 13.

[13]Grenz, *Primer*, p. 14.

[14]Webber, *Younger Evangelicals*, p. 69.

[15]Long, *Emerging Hope*, pp. 77, 78.

[16]Grenz, *Primer*, p. 38.

[17]Middleton and Walsh, *Truth Is Stranger*, p. 39.

[18]Webber, *Younger Evangelicals*, p. 53.

[19]Grenz, *Primer*, pp. 14, 20.

[20]Grenz, *Primer*, pp. 42, 43.

[21]Brian McLaren, *A New Kind of Christian* (San Francisco: Jossey-Bass, 2001), pp. 60-67.

[22]Long, *Emerging Hope*, p. 63.

[23]Andy Crouch, "The Emergent Mystique," *Christianity Today*, November 2004, p. 37.

[24]For the list of speakers for the 2005 event see <web.archive.org/web/ 20041120005848/www.emergentconvention.com/2005/convention_info/ speakers.php>. For the list of speakers for the 2008 event see: <www.thegreat emergence.com/TheEvent>.

[25]"And He never said a mumblin' word," May 11, 2008 <http://princessmax .blogspot.com/2008/05/and-he-never-said-mumblin-word.html>.

[26]Middleton and Walsh, *Truth Is Stranger,* p. 13.

[27]Phone interview with Anthony Smith (August 15, 2008).

[28]Grenz, *Primer,* p. 133.

[29]Ibid., pp. 131-34, See also Paul Rabinow, ed., "Introduction," in *The Foucault Reader* (New York: Pantheon, 1984), pp. 6-7; and Michel Foucault, "Nietzsche, Genealogy, History," in *The Postmodernism Reader: Foundational Texts*, ed. Michael Drolet (New York: Routledge, 2004), pp. 72-85.

[30]Grenz, *Primer,* 161.

[31]Middleton and Walsh, *Truth Is Stranger,* p. 188.

[32]Bolger and Gibbs, *Emerging Churches,* pp. 239-328. The bios of key "emerging" church leaders reveal a high number of former Southern Baptists and disaffected pastors leaving Baby Boomer megachurches.

[33]Brian McLaren, "Out of the Echo Chamber," *Leadership* 28, no. 1 (2007): 110.

[34]"And He never said a mumblin' word," online posting (May 14, 2008) Wild Rumpus <princessmax.blogspot.com/2008_05_01_archive.html>.

Chapter 6: The Cultural Imperialism of the Western, White Captivity of the Church

[1]Jean Baudrillard, *Simulacra and Simulation*, trans. Sheila Faria Glaser (Ann Arbor: University of Michigan Press, 1994), p. 21.

[2]Joel Stein, "A New Fast-Food Invasion," *Time*, March 29, 2007 <http://www .time.com/time/magazine/article/0,9171,1604946,00.html>.

[3]Thomas L. Friedman, *The Lexus and the Olive Tree* (New York: Farrar, Straus and Giroux, 1999), pp. xiii, 7-8.

[4]Ibid., p. 8.

[5]Ibid., p. 35.

[6]Based upon phone surveys of Bangkok area Bible colleges conducted by a Thai pastor.

[7]Philip Jenkins, *The Next Christendom* (New York: Oxford University Press, 2002), p. 3.

[8]Barrett and Johnson, *Christian Trends*, p. 615.

[9]Simona Grigore, "The Roma (Gypsy) Community in Bucharest, Romania," <http://www.lausanneworldpulse.com/urban.php/840/10-2007?pg=all>.

[10]Isaac Phiri and Joe Maxwell, "Gospel Riches: Africa's rapid embrace of prosperity Pentecostalism provokes concern—and hope," *Christianity Today*, July 2007, p. 24.

[11]Ibid., p. 23.

[12]Nancy R. Pearcey, *Total Truth: Liberating Christianity from Its Cultural Captivity* (Wheaton, Ill.: Crossway, 2004), p. 47.

[13]Andrew Walls, *The Missionary Movement in Christian History* (Maryknoll, N.Y.: Orbis, 1996), pp. 43-44.

[14]See <http://www.urbana.org/u2006.mediaplayer.pop.cfm?gotosession=3&clip=132> for the audio or video clip from Urbana 06.

[15]Lamin Sanneh, *Translating the Message: The Missionary Impact on Culture* (Maryknoll, N.Y.: Orbis, 1989), pp. 2, 4.

[16]Ibid., p. 3.

[17]Walls, *Missionary Movement*, pp. 27-28.

[18]Ibid., p. 47.

[19]F. F. Bruce, *The Book of the Acts*, The New International Commentary on the New Testament (Grand Rapids: Eerdmans, 1988), p. 286.

Chapter 7: Suffering and Celebration

[1]R. Kent Hughes, *Romans: Righteousness from Heaven* (Wheaton, Ill.: Crossway, 1991), p. 232.

[2]Walter Brueggemann, *Peace* (St. Louis: Chalice, 2001), p. 29.

[3]I am indebted to Dr. Humberto Alfaro for introducing me to Walter Brueggemann's concepts of *suffering* and *celebration*.

[4]Ron Mitchell, *Organic Faith* (Chicago: Cornerstone, 1998), p. 26.

[5]Richard Sennett, *Flesh and Stone* (New York: W. W. Norton, 1994), p. 374.

[6]James M. Jasper, *A Restless Nation* (Chicago: University of Chicago Press, 2000), p. 69.

[7]Sennett, *Flesh and Stone*, pp. 255, 256.

[8]An additional aspect of mobility is how current global factors and the U.S. government's role in global politics can shape the forced movement of people. For example, the Vietnam War caused the displacement of Vietnamese, Cambodians and Lao-

tians, which led to the influx of Southeast Asian immigration. In the same way, another aspect of forced mobility includes the colonization of Africa, which led to numerous geopolitical complexities leading to numerous civil wars, the African diaspora and even genocide. Another aspect is the doctrine of Manifest Destiny, which led to the border crossing of Mexico and the expulsion of Mexicans from their native lands for the benefit of America's quest for the Western coastal border.

[9]Jim Wallis, *The Soul of Politics* (New York: New Press/Orbis, 1994), pp. 5, 40.

[10]Ray Bakke, *The Urban Christian* (Downers Grove, Ill.: InterVarsity Press, 1987), p. 59.

[11]Brueggemann, *Peace*, p. 35.

[12]Richard Twiss, *One Church, Many Tribes* (Ventura, Calif.: Regal, 2000), p. 58.

[13]Ibid., p. 39. See also John Dawson, *Healing America's Wounds* (Ventura, Calif.: Regal, 1977), pp. 135-59; and Dee Brown, *Bury My Heart at Wounded Knee* (New York: Henry Holt, 1970).

[14]Randy Woodley, *Living in Color* (Downers Grove, Ill.: InterVarsity Press, 2001), p. 18.

[15]Twiss, *One Church*, p. 40.

[16]Edward Gilbreath, *Reconciliation Blues* (Downers Grove, Ill.: InterVarsity Press, 2006), pp. 40-41.

[17]C. Eric Lincoln and Lawrence H. Mamiya, *The Black Church in the African American Experience* (Durham, N.C.: Duke University Press, 1990), p. xi.

[18]The lyrics are from the following songs: "The Heart of Worship" by Matt Redman; "Trading My Sorrows" by Darrell Evans; "Hungry" by Kathryn Scott; and "Blessed Be Your Name" by Matt Redman.

[19]Lincoln and Mamiya, *Black Church*, pp. 350, 352.

[20]Albert J. Raboteau, *Slave Religion: The "Invisible Institution" in the Antebellum South* (New York: Oxford University Press, 1978), p. 251. See also James Cone, *The Spirituals and the Blues* (New York: Seabury, 1972).

[21]Lincoln and Mamiya, *Black Church*, p. 158.

[22]Ibid., p. 347.

[23]Harold J. Recinos, *Good News from the Barrio: Prophetic Witness for the Church* (Louisville: Westminster John Knox, 2006), p. 5.

[24]See Peggy McIntosh, "Unpacking the Invisible Knapsack" in Rothenberg, *White Privilege*, pp. 97-101.

Chapter 8: Holistic Evangelism

[1]"The total number of Koreans in the United States was estimated at less than

fifty before the first large wave of Korean immigrants reached the Hawaiian shores during the period 1903-1905. The history of Korean immigration to America thus began in 1903" (Won Moo Hurh and Kwang Chung Kim, *Korean Immigrants in America* [Rutherford, N.J.: Fairleigh Dickinson University Press, 1984], p. 39).

[2]Hurh and Kim, *Korean Immigrants,* p. 53.

[3]Jessica S. Barnes and Claudette E. Bennett, "The Asian Population: 2000" (Washington D.C.: U.S. Department of Commerce, Economics and Statistics Administration, 2002). Available online at <http://www.census.gov/prod/2002 pubs/c2kbr01-16.pdf>.

[4]Pyong Gap Min, "The Structures and Social Functions of Korean Immigrant Churches in the United States," *International Migration Review* 26, no. 4 (1989): 1376. Won Moo Hurh and Kwang Chung Kim, "Religious Participation of Korean Immigrants in the United States," *Journal for the Scientific Study of Religion* 29, no. 1 (1990): 24.

[5]Hyung-chan Kim, "History and Role of the Church in the Korean American Community," in *The Koreans in America 1882-1974,* ed. Hyung-chan Kim and Wayne Patterson (New York: Oceana, 1974), p. 134.

[6]Min, "Structures and Social Functions," p. 1377; and Hurh and Kim, "Religious Participation," p. 19.

[7]"Although only a little more than 20 percent of Koreans are affiliated with Christian churches in Korea, the majority of Korean immigrants in the United States have had a Christian background in their home country. For example, in a survey of the 1986 cohort of Korean immigrants conducted in Seoul before emigration, 54 percent of the respondents reported that they were affiliated with Protestant or Catholic churches" (Min, "Structures and Social Functions," p. 1376).

[8]Ibid., p. 1380.

[9]A survey of Korean Americans conducted in 1984 revealed that "the great majority (68.7%) preferred the Korean ethnic church over the American church. . . . Through the foregoing observations, it becomes apparent that the Korean immigrant's attachment to their native culture and society is generally strong" (Hurh and Kim, "Religious Participation," p. 79).

[10]Hurh and Kim, *Korean Immigrants,* p. 133.

[11]C. Eric Lincoln and Lawrence H. Mamiya, *The Black Church in the African American Experience* (Durham, N.C.: Duke University Press, 1990), p. 17.

[12]Min, "Structures and Social Functions," p. 1376.

[13]Ibid., p. 1371.

[14]Hurh and Kim, *Korean Immigrants,* p. 91.

[15]Ibid., p. 88.

[16]Min, "Structures and Social Functions," p. 1372.

[17]Kim, "History and Role," p. 137.

[18]Ibid., pp. 1377-79.

[19]Hurh and Kim, "Religious Participation," p. 30.

[20]Min, "Structures and Social Functions," p. 1385.

[21]Hurh and Kim, *Korean Immigrants,* p. 95.

[22]Min, "Structures and Social Functions," p. 1389.

[23]See Min, "Structures and Social Functions," p. 1374; and Hurh and Kim, *Korean Immigrants*, p. 129.

[24]Min, "Structures and Social Functions," p. 1374.

[25]Hurh and Kim, "Religious Participation," p. 32.

[26]"Most Korean churches in the United States do not have their own buildings. Instead, they usually have service and fellowship meetings in American churches" (Min, "Structures and Social Functions," p. 1378). American churches can view this generous support for Korean immigrant churches as a missionary effort, geared toward reaching a foreign people.

Chapter 9: A Multicultural Worldview

[1]W. E. B. DuBois, *The Souls of Black Folk*, in Three Negro Classics (New York: Avon, 1965), p. 215.

[2]Eldin Villafañe, *The Liberating Spirit.* (Grand Rapids: Eerdmans, 1993), p. 23.

[3]The Korean term for second-generation Korean Americans.

[4]Kenneth Uyeda Fong, *Insights for Growing Asian-American Ministries* (Rosemead, Calif.: EverGrowing, 1990), p. 46.

[5]Villafañe, *Liberating Spirit*, p. 21.

[6]Isidro Lucas, *The Browning of America: The Hispanic Revolution in the American Church* (Chicago: Fides / Claretian, 1981), p. 7.

[7]Villafañe, *Liberating Spirit*, p. 21. See also Virgilio Elizondo, *Galilean Journey: The Mexican-American Promise* (Maryknoll, N.Y.: Orbis, 1983), pp. 5, 18, 19.

[8]Philip Jenkins, *The Next Christendom* (New York: Oxford University Press, 2002), p. 116.

[9]David R. Harris and Jeremiah Joseph Sim, "Who Is Multiracial? Assessing the Complexity of Lived Race," *American Sociological Review* 67, no. 4 (August 2002): 614.

[10]David C. Pollock and Ruth E. Van Reken, *Third Culture Kids: The Experience of Growing Up Among Worlds* (Yarmouth, Maine: Intercultural, 1999), p. 6.

[11]Harold Augenbraum and Ilan Stavans, eds., *Growing Up Latino: Memoirs and Stories* (New York: Houghton Mifflin, 1993).

[12]Fumitaka Matsuoka, *Out of Silence: Emerging Themes in Asian American Churches* (Cleveland: United Church Press, 1995).

[13]Chang-Rae Lee, *Native Speaker* (New York: Riverhead, 1995), p. 12.

[14]Ibid., p. 7.

[15]A completely inaccurate statement given how many times news reports led off with the statement about Cho's national identity. In contrast, when a similar massacre was caused in early 2008 on the campus of Northern Illinois University by a white student, there was little or no mention of his racial identity.

[16]Patrick J. Buchanan, "The Dark Side of Diversity," May 1, 2007 <http://www.buchanan.org/blog/?p=731>.

[17]Dowell Myers, *Immigrants and Boomers* (New York: Russell Sage Foundation, 2007), p. 6.

[18]Harold J. Recinos, *Good News from the Barrio: Prophetic Witness for the Church* (Louisville: Westminster John Knox, 2006), p. 27. See also David Bacon, "Immigrants: Are Undocumented Workers Being Thrown to the Wolves?" <http://www.igc.apc.org/dbacon/Imgrants/12split.html>.

[19]See David T. Olson, *The American Church in Crisis* (Grand Rapids: Zondervan, 2008).

[20]Doug Hall and Judy Hall, *A Culture of Hope* (unpublished manuscript), p. 82.

[21]Myers, *Immigrants*, p. 11.

[22]Ibid., pp. 8-9.

[23]Andrew F. Walls, *The Cross-Cultural Process in Christian History* (Maryknoll, N.Y.: Orbis, 2002), p. 81.

[24]Eric Gorski, "Hispanic churches add English services," *USA Today*, August 23, 2007 <http://www.usatoday.com/news/religion/2007-08-23-744772130_x.htm>.

[25]Ibid.

Conclusion

[1]Richard Kyle, *Evangelicalism: An Americanized Christianity* (New Brunswick, N.J.: Transaction, 2006), p. 313.

[2]David Anderson, *Gracism* (Downers Grove, Ill.: InterVarsity Press, 2007), p. 40.

[3]Ibid., pp. 40-41.

[4]For more on the story and to see the actual excerpts, see <http://www

.christianitytoday.com/todayschristian/special/speakingup.html>.

[5]Mark Oestreicher, "A Public Apology to Our Asian American Brothers and Sisters," online posting (March 2, 2007) YSMARKO <http://www.ysmarko .com/?p=1379>.

Name and Subject Index

Scripture Index